JN302471

Feudalism

A Comparative Study

Feudalism. Capitalism. Sovereignty.

What is feudalism? Addressing the theories put forward to date and comparing historically feudal societies, the author constructs a universal, appropriate "ideal" type of feudalism. He probes factors behind the formation of feudal systems and the driving forces behind modern capitalism, and solves the conundrum of transcendent sovereignty, including Japan's Emperor system. He seeks answers to these issues using references from Western Europe, Japan, China and Egypt.

Feudalism

A Comparative Study

Naohiko Tonomura

Translated by
Robert A. Mintzer

ASAHI PRESS

3-3-5 NISHI-KANDA, CHIYODA-KU, TOKYO 101-0065, JAPAN

TELEPHONE 81-3-3263-3321

ISBN978-4-255-00599-7　C0082

©Naohiko Tonomura 2011, Printed in Japan

Copyright 2011. All rights reserved

Contents

FOREWORD 7

CHAPTER ONE
   A Comparative Study of Feudalism
   — In search of a unified concept of feudalism — 11

CHAPTER TWO
   The Formation of Feudalism 95

CHAPTER THREE
   Transition from Feudalism to Capitalism 123

CHAPTER FOUR
   Transcendent Sovereignty 185

Outline of Japanese History 247
Bibliography 248
About the Author 254

FOREWORD

In studying feudal society, I felt a strong attraction to this society and era. Could it be because in doing so I am taken vicariously into a society that, until as recently as roughly a hundred years ago, my ancestors lived in for centuries, a society whose remnant structures still exist all around me? Yes, this is surely part of the attraction, but on deeper reflection there is definitely more to it.

To people today, feudal societies often seem incomprehensible societies of entirely negative worth. They are typically characterized by rigidly fixed social status, undeveloped systems of transportation and communication, a narrow sphere of activity, a low standard of living, inadequate medical care and a short life expectancy. But is feudalism a type of rule chosen freely by a ruler, of his own volition, from among many possibilities? This may be the prevailing assumption, but the reality, I would suggest, is that a ruler was offered no latitude of choice within the broad framework of history's flow, but rather was able to make modifications only in terms of details, and feudalism was, in anyone's eyes, the best social configuration available at the time in question. Moreover, although feudal societies had their inconveniences and hardships, when measured against the yardstick of the society or its history and not against the yardstick of the individual, they may in fact for that reason have had some positive worth. This is a sentiment that often crosses my mind in the course of my research.

While this is a major issue in the history of mankind that to date has not been fully addressed, it is not my focus here. What I address in this book are but a number of issues within the conventional framework of theories expounded on the subject of feudalism. What follows below is a brief introduction to those issues.

The word "feudalism" is used in two senses: in the traditional, legal historical sense and in the Marxian, economic historical sense. In this work I focus my discussion on the former while simultaneously also addressing interpretation of the latter. Examples of feudal societies in the legal historical sense are Japan, Western Europe and China. Although occasionally the societies of Egypt, Byzantium, the Islamic world and Russia are also cited, owing to the ambiguity of feudalism's conceptual stipulations opinions vary from one scholar to another, with some admitting the presence of feudalism only within Western European society and no others. In order to achieve a unified understanding within the debate on feudalism, it is therefore necessary to begin by bringing unity to these multiple concepts.

In chapter 1, "A Comparative Study of Feudalism," in a quest to reach a unified concept I will attempt, by considering the definitions offered by various experts and specific examples of feudal societies, to configure an objective and appropriate "ideal" type of feudalism that

FOREWORD

does not lean toward any one specific society.

In chapter 2, "The Formation of Feudalism," based on the conclusion reached in chapter 1, I will seek one factor common to the formation of numerous feudal societies. I will do so while taking under consideration the view on the formation of feudalism advanced by Otto Hintze.

In chapter 3, "Transition from Feudalism to Capitalism," I will probe the fundamental forces that crushed feudalism and gave birth to a modern capitalist society. By comparing the economies and societies of ancient Rome, Han-dynasty China and Japan in the late Edo Period, I will attempt to indicate a new interpretation different from the conventional one.

In chapter 4, "Transcendent Sovereignty," I will seek out reasons that enabled feudal monarchs — in the case of Japan, the Emperors — while losing their real political power, to maintain their absolute authority for hundreds of years. Through comparisons of multiple examples of transcendent sovereignty, I will attempt to find a new answer to this conundrum.

The present volume is a complete translation of my book Hikaku hōkenseiron [Comparative Feudalism] published in its original Japanese-language edition in 1991. For many years now, this work has served as a textbook in courses on Western history taught at numerous Japanese universities, including the Graduate School of the University of Tokyo, and therefore it has been widely studied by many students. This English translation was made possible with the able assistance of Robert A. Mintzer, to whom I wish to express my deep appreciation. I would also like to thank Masahisa Hara, president of Asahi Press, for his kind cooperation in publishing this book, and also Hisayo Sato of Asahi Press for her valuable help in enabling the smooth execution of the translation process.

Autumn 2010

Naohiko Tonomura

CHAPTER ONE

A Comparative Study of Feudalism

— In search of a unified concept of feudalism —

1

Introduction

As is widely known, the concept of "feudalism" today is broadly used in two different senses: one being a system integrating a vassalage system with a system of enfeoffment, the other being a serfdom system. Whereas the former meaning is a concept of legal history expressing the legal order of a dominant class, the latter is a concept of economic history, primarily drawn from Marxian economics, with a focus on direct producers, i.e. those of a dominated status. Within these two usages, moreover, each has its own differentiated uses, and on occasion one finds the same individual using the term "feudalism" on differing levels of meaning. Inherently, however, the concept of feudalism is singular, and it is not merely desirable but arguably even necessary to restore unity of some type that is fully capable of functioning to differentiate among social forms and to remove abuses arising from multiplicity of meaning.

The Japanese word for "feudalism" is *hōkensei* 封建制. The origin of the word traces to the feudal system, or *fengjian-zhidu* 封建制度, of China's Zhou Dynasty (1045-256 BCE). The *Zuo Zhuan* (Chronicle of Zuo: 636 BCE) states, "In olden times the Duke of Zhou enfeoffed his relatives and thereby enclosed the House of Zhou." The first character in the compound, *feng*, signifies the granting of land; the second character, *jian*, means to build the state. According to *Han Shu* (Book of Han: 111 CE), the number of fiefs in early Zhou times reached 800, of which more than 50 belonged to the Zhou royal family. Of the remaining 750, a modest number were granted to meritorious retainers while the bulk were accorded to the powerful families of each region. The *Han Shu* goes on to say that the House of Zhou granted them territorial sovereignty and thus made them serve to protect the royal lands "one thousand *li* square" centered on the capital, the "heavenly domain." During Qin Dynasty times (221-206 BCE), the framework of princely feudalism was abandoned and replaced by a system of centrally controlled commanderies and districts, and thereafter in China the terms for "feudalism" (*fengjianzhi*) and "commandery-district system" (*junxianzhi*) were continuously used in diametrically opposed senses.

In Japan, the term *hōkensei* was not used in antiquity, and in native historical works such as *Gukanshō* (ca. 1220) and *Jinnō Shōtōki* (14th C) the phrases *musha no yo* (age of warriors) and buke no yo (age of military houses) referred to feudal times. From the middle of the Edo Period (1603-1868), the word *hōkensei* then gradually came to be used among Confucian scholars and gained firm ground that continued into the Meiji Period (1868-1912). Afterward, from the Meiji Period onward, in view of its similarities with the feudalism of the West — the systems of vassalage and fiefdoms, etc. — *hōkensei* has been used also as the Japanese translation of the English word "feudalism."

The Western term "feudalism" originates from the Frankish word *fehu-od*, meaning "livestock" or "valuable property." This transmuted to signify conferred immovable property, i.e. feudal landholdings, and from the 10th century came to be widely used in such forms as *fevum* or *feodum*. Use of the word "feudalism" to express a social system as a whole was not seen during the Middle Ages; it began to be used ambiguously by jurists in the 17th century to express a form of land ownership, but then in the 18th century, from around the time of the French Revolution, in the revolutionary sweep to break with the old systems "feudalism" came to be widely used with negative overtones. *Lehenswesen*, the term used in Germany, has the same connotation as "feudalism," i.e.

a system of enfeoffment.

Two Standpoints

Whether making reference to the Japanese word *hōkensei* or the English "feudalism," those who take the stand of a legal historical interpretation, which sees feudalism as an integration of vassalage and enfeoffment systems, contend their view is justified by the foregoing traditional linguistic usages. Moreover, they contend that the concept of feudalism that centers on the exploited—the producers or serfs—has too broad a range of applications and is thus not useful for historical analysis. Joseph Strayer, for example, says that a serf-based mode of production not only can be found in the West during the Middle Ages but was also carried out during both the preceding and subsequent periods—and even in modern industrialized societies. He states that a definition of feudalism that encompasses the systems of the ancient Middle East, the Late Roman Empire, medieval Europe, the American south in the 19th century and the Soviet Union in the 1930s "is not much use."

By contrast, people who take a Marxist view of history, which lays stress on production or class relations (serfdom), actually play up the comprehensiveness of the concept and the broad range of its applications. Keiji Nagahara states that since a legal historic perspective deals only with the collective form of the dominant class, this in itself cannot be taken as the entirety of social relationships. He contends that a view based on mode of production includes not only particulars applying to farmers and farm operators but also matters concerning landowners and power structure, and for this reason it is a more comprehensive categorization. He further adds that if one assumes that systems of vassalage and enfeoffment developed to the extent of permeating throughout society only in Western Europe and Japan, then it is inappropriate to make this a theoretical framework for feudalism in the context of all racial and national histories.

Weakness of the Economic Historical Concept

Insofar as the two matters in question — the concept's comprehensiveness and its breadth of application range — are concerned, however, the economic historical concept is not necessarily advantageous in the way Nagahara suggests.

To begin, it is not necessarily the case that the concept of feudalism centering on dominated serfs is the more comprehensive since it also includes matters pertaining to those in the dominating position. This is because the concept focused on lord-vassal relationships and enfeoffment by the dominant class also innately includes the living modes of the dominated class and ownership modes. Understanding the entirety of social relationships is not possible or impossible depending on the standpoint; it is inherent in both viewpoints and by its nature emerges according to the stance of the researcher.

As to the breadth of each concept's range of applications, here there is a clear difference: the perception centering on serfdom tends to expand too broadly, and the perspective based around vassalage and enfeoffment tends to become too narrow. If the central focus is taken to be the production relationship and class struggle between landowners and small farmers, then even in the case of China alone, we find feudalism present not only during the Zhou Dynasty but also in Qin and Han (202 BCE-220 CE) days when the system of commanderies and districts prevailed, as well as in the subsequent Sui (581-618), Tang (618-907), Song (960-1279), Yuan (1279-1368), Ming (1368-1644) and Qing (1644-1911) eras. For a fact, in contemporary China history is divided according to two methods: (1) early feudal society (Western Zhou Dynasty [ca. 1040-771 BCE] until unification under the Qin); middle feudal society, early phase (Qin until unification under the Sui); middle feudal society, later phase (Sui through to the end of Yuan); and late feudal society (Ming and Qing); and (2) early and late feudal periods spanning the entirety of Chinese history, the line of division drawn in the middle of the Tang Dynasty. In the case of Japan also, there is thus nothing strange in attributing feudalism to the periods that predate the Kamakura Era (1185-1333), which marks the start of feudalism in the conventional view: the Heian (794-1185), Nara (710-794), and even the Tumulus Period (ca. 220-552). This being the case, the term "feudal" can be applied to a fair number of societies in world history before our modern civil and industrialized society — a period of only some one or two hundred years — including some that stretch over a thousand or two thousand years. As such, it can hardly be said to be an effective conceptual apparatus for undertaking social analysis.

Those who embrace this way of thinking say that because the concept of feudalism based on vassalage and enfeoffment is not applicable to societies other than those of Japan and Western Europe, it cannot be said to be universal; however, this criticism is not necessarily on the mark. Why? Because this thinking is based on the preconception that the concept of feudalism should be sweepingly applicable over extremely long periods of world history and vast geographic areas. But inherently feudalism is not a concept having such grand demands. Also, even outside Japan and Western Europe we can find any number of societies that take forms close to theirs.

Weakness of the Legal Historical Concept

The legal historical concept has its weak point, too,

however. Namely, the legal historical concept tends, in direct opposition to the economic historical concept's tendency toward abstraction, toward specificity; and as the conceptual level approaches specificity and the conceptual stipulations become correspondingly precise, the range of applications narrows until, ultimately, it can potentially designate a specific situation. In reality, this "specific situation" is Western European feudalism, and indeed this is often treated as feudalism itself.

In the 18th century Montesquieu, the first person to apply the term "feudalism" to the social form of medieval Europe, stated that feudalism is a phenomenon that had occurred only once in all the world and would likely never occur again in the future. Contrastingly, Voltaire, Montesquieu's contemporary, contended that feudalism is an extremely old social form that in his own time continued to exist in three-quarters of the Northern Hemisphere. As the world became increasingly knowledgeable, it was the thinking of Voltaire that came to be accepted as correct. Especially, when it was discovered that an example of feudalism closely resembling that of Europe existed in Japan, an extremely distant culture, this was nothing but astounding to Europeans. Still, this generalization of feudalism was a notion that, through the 19th and 20th centuries, Europeans were somehow unable to accept, accompanied by feelings of vague discomfort. Time and again the contention was repeated that European feudalism was the genuine article and that feudalism as found in Japan and elsewhere was a special form and not "the real thing."

"The feudalism discussed here, it must be emphasized, was a system peculiar to western Europe and was not found elsewhere except in a few regions of the Mediterranean and the Middle East, where it was introduced for a time by the Crusaders. This does not mean that there were not feudal systems in other areas of the world, but that western feudalism was quite different from Byzantine, Moslem, Japanese, and Chinese feudalism."
— Bryce Lyon

"The classical age of feudalism is usually dated from the eleventh to the thirteenth centuries and located in northern France. Other societies in different historical periods, whether European or non-European, are compared to this northern French society to determine the extent to which feudal institutions and tendencies developed within them."
— J. Prawer & S. Eisenstadt

"Some other societies had some of these characteristics, and one other society, Japan from 1300 to 1600, had most of them. But feudalism appeared first and developed most completely in Western Europe between 800 and 1200."
— Joseph Strayer

"The only remedy for these uncertainties is to go back to

the origins of the problem. Since it is obvious that all these societies, separated by time and space, have received the name 'feudal' only on account of their similarities, real or supposed, to Western feudalism, it is the characteristics of this basic type, to which all the others must be referred, that it is of primary importance to define."

—— Marc Bloch

Thus, it has been said, somewhat peculiarly, that feudalism is unique to Europe but also exists elsewhere; or that European feudalism is the classic example and complete, and therefore others must conform to it; or that feudalism first appeared in Europe and other systems are called "feudal" simply because they resemble European feudalism, therefore suggesting that only European feudalism is "first-class" and all others are of dubious nature and "second-class." While it is likely Europe's self-righteous hegemonism that lurks beneath such discriminatory views, what in the end prevented the ultimate eventuation in that direction—the formation of a proper noun, "Feudalism" with a capital "F"—was the existence of feudalism in Japan so closely resembling the European system. Japanese feudalism truly struck like a "bolt out of the blue," wielding a crushing blow to European ambitions of global conquest. "If we conclude that Japan was feudal," wrote John Whitney Hall, "we must do so with the full realization that Japan *became feudal independently of Europe.* This is the kind of thought that seems either to excite or revolt the historian."

Polarization

In this manner, the two concepts of feudalism — one diffusing into a universal abstraction and approaching an infinite range of applications, the other concentrated on a single entity and dwindling to no range of applications — are moving in opposite directions, and both are losing their usefulness as a means of historical analysis. What gave these two directions to this static concept inherently devoid of magnetic fields were on the one hand the magnetic pole of Marxist political ideology, and on the other hand the magnetic pole of what are now called "ethnic feelings" lurking within the European subconscience. "Feudalism" cannot serve as a useful means of analyzing history unless it is a concept that is liberated from the pull of these two magnetic fields and is magnetically void, detached and objective.

How then is such a concept to be obtained? To be frank, I would like to speak of "one" concept here. But to reconcile and unify these two major categories so distantly apart, each operating without concern for the other, is in the end a total impossibility, and thus is a task we likely have no choice but to abandon. What we can do is to limit ourselves to just one or the other, and here my intention is to address only the concept in the category of legal history. However, given that the legal historical category is the inherent parent body of the concept of feudalism as well as the category which is the mainstream within European historical studies, and, in light of the murkiness and opacity of the current situation as well as the strong tendency toward individual specificity, I can declare with conviction that the establishment of clear, objective and unified rules is in itself a task having great significance. For my immediate purposes, I will set aside the Marxian economic historical concept.

Hall's Attempt

To my knowledge, only one scholar has attempted to grapple squarely with the task of achieving a unified concept of feudalism in the realm of legal history: John Whitney Hall.

In an article titled "Feudalism in Japan – A Reassessment" (1962), Hall states that feudalism is an ideal type of human organization straddling multiple cultures. He states that in determining an ideal type, it does not suffice to rely solely on the "whim or imagination" of a single historian; what is vital is to undertake a process of hypothesis verification based on empirical data, working through cultural comparisons and comparisons of other social situations to determine the variables that are the component elements of the feudalism type, set the limits to those variables, and precisely define what is at the essence. Hall then contends that the foremost reason why conventional historical research has repeatedly failed to reach a definition of feudalism is because historians have failed to make systematic efforts in that regard.

But Hall, perhaps owing to the theme of his article — a reassessment of Japanese feudalism — in practice indicates no conclusive explanation. From the various definitions of feudalism offered to date (Wittfogel, Weber, Maitland, Levy, Lenin, Asakawa) he extracts three essential elements of feudalism: within the political sector, the "lord-vassal complex"; in the social sector, the "social status system"; and within the economic sector, "self-sufficiency." As his own definition deriving from these three elements, Hall goes no further than attempting to clarify that in this light the feudalism of Japan possesses the essential traits of feudalism. Hall's definition is too simply reached: he makes no mention of feudal societies other than those of Europe and Japan, makes no comparisons among component elements, and undertakes no matching against empirical data. In other words he does not construct an ideal type.

My Plan

Like Hall, I think of feudalism as an ideal type, one category of human organization straddling multiple cultures, and I believe that, by forming a hypothesis and verifying it using empirical data, it is possible to clarify that ideal type. This is what I will do in practice in the following pages, proceeding in this order: first, I will review a number of definitions of feudalism offered until now, and I will select items that appear to have given shape to earlier concepts of feudalism; next, using those items as my guiding markers, I will address the circumstances of all societies to date considered to have been feudal, and I will undertake a comparative study of them; and third, based on that study I will extract component elements while determining their relative weight, and construct an ideal type.

In the case of well-worn concepts like feudalism, attempts at definition are not allowed to be undertaken freely with no regard for customary usages long in use. Only when such usages are studied and successively investigated — a time-consuming process — has it been deemed possible to achieve results. The problem lies in what has constituted the real nexus of the concept. What I aim to do here is to find that nexus among various sundry items of secondary and tertiary nature, to extract it, polish it, "dress" it in new attire, and make a fresh start using it as a useful weapon for subdividing history.

2

Asakawa's View

The various theories on feudalism I will introduce here are, in chronological order, those of Kan'ichi Asakawa, Max Weber, Otto Hintze, Joseph Strayer and John Whitney Hall. As points of reference I will also describe Lenin's take on Marxist economic history and the view of Keiji Nagahara. All of these individuals, to one extent or another, defined feudalism drawing on multicultural sources. I will not address the definitions of those who dealt with the feudal system peculiar to one specific culture: for example, Joseph Calmette, Marc Bloch or François-Louis Ganshof.

"Some Aspects of Japanese Feudal Institutions," published in English by Kan'ichi Asakawa (1873-1948) in 1918, is an article comparing Japanese feudalism to the feudal system of Europe. It is one of only a few studies that for a long time served as a source of information pertaining to Japanese feudalism for Europeans.

In this work Asakawa poses the question, "What is feudalism?"; and as its characteristic traits he offers up the following three points:

1) The ruling class should consist of groups of fighting men, each group chained together by links of an exhaustive personal bond of mutual service.
2) The private land law of this society should recog-

nize no absolute ownership, only a series of relative tenures.
3) There should result private usurpation of public rights and public utilization of private institutions; i.e., in government, in finance, in military affairs, and in the administration of justice, there should be a complete confusion or coalescence of the public and the private.

As circumstances necessary for the development of a feudal system having these traits, Asakawa offers that a society must meet the following three conditions:
1) It should have organized itself into a more or less centralized state, and at the same time retain its memory of that older mode of life in which kinship was the controlling bond of society.
2) It should definitely be in what has been termed the stage of "land economy," so that there should be, in relation to the population, scarcity of money in circulation and abundance of land for agricultural uses.
3) Social unrest should persist during a sufficiently long period (about six centuries in the cases both of Europe and of Japan) to enable the private relations to make such progressive adjustments that finally their two sides — namely, land and armed service — should penetrate into each other and be beaten into a unique system of social organization.

Asakawa contends that in the history of the world it

is anomalous for all three conditions to be met, and this fluke has occurred only among few peoples — in Europe and Japan.

Weber's View

Max Weber (1864-1920), as is widely known, differentiated three forms of domination: charismatic domination, traditional domination and legal-rational domination. He contended that whereas charismatic domination stems from an emotional belief in a leader's extraordinary powers — especially his mystical capabilities and heroic words and deeds — and legal-rational domination is bureaucratic domination based on objectively formulated rules, traditional domination derives from belief in the sanctity of the social order and dominant authority in existence since antiquity. Weber suggested that there are two types of traditional domination: a purely patriarchal structure of despotic domination by a single ruler, and a status-based structure of domination by a small number of rulers who have independent status and hold official positions but who share their authority with an overlord. Sultanism is representative of the former type, Weber offered, and feudalism is typical of the latter.

Feudalism, in the broadest sense, is a combination of granting of lands and mandatory military service. Weber said it existed in various types:

1) Liturgic feudalism: soldiers provided with land, frontier guards
2) Patrimonial feudalism
   a) Levies of peasant farmers (*coloni*) (ancient Rome and Egypt)
   b) Slaves (ancient Babylonia, Egypt, medieval Arabia)
   c) Hereditary clients as private soldiers (Roman nobility)
3) Free feudalism
   a) Vassalic: only by virtue of personal fealty, without the granting of manorial rights (Japan, Merovingian *trustis*)
   b) Prebendal: without personal fealty, only by virtue of granted manorial rights and tax revenues (Middle East)
   c) Feudatory: personal fealty and enfeoffment combined (Occident)
   d) Urban: warriors, based on manorial land allotted to the individual (Hellenic polis of the Spartan type)

Among these, Weber attached the greatest importance to free feudalism, which he considered as genuine feudalism, especially that of the feudatory type; he viewed the prebendal type as "next-most genuine."

Weber described feudatory free feudalism as having the following five characteristics:

1) Granting of lands normally based on military ser-

vice, and sometimes on government service
2) Reciprocal contract between free individuals based on fidelity
3) Theoretically, a purely personal lifelong contract; in practice, hereditary contract renewal
4) Status-based hierarchy
5) Special chivalrous lifestyle supported by feelings of honor

In prebendal free feudalism, benefices (prebend) are granted not to individuals but, on a non-hereditary basis, to performers of official duties. In the sense of being objective, prebendal feudalism is closely akin to bureaucracy; and Weber contended that it lacks a contract based in fealty, feelings of honor, and a chivalrous lifestyle.

Although prebendal feudalism thus differs from feudatory feudalism in many ways, Weber considered it a form of genuine feudalism. By contrast, he did not include vassalic feudalism among forms of genuine feudalism despite the fact that, although it does not entail the granting of manorial rights, it contains elements of militarism, individual personality, occasions of fidelity, and a chivalrous lifestyle within a lord-vassal relationship. Weber's exclusion owed to his emphasis, among the various characteristics listed, on the granting of lands based on military service and contracts between free individuals.

Hintze's View

Otto Hintze (1861-1940), a disciple of Weber, described the feudalism of Western Europe as having the following three characteristics (*Wesen und Verbreitung des Feudalismus* [Essence and Diffusion of Feudalism], 1929):

1) Vassalage and enfeoffment of professional warriors (military function)
2) Manorial system of peasant farmers serving lords (socio-economic function)
3) Fragmentation of political power among local secular and non-secular lords (political function).

In Hintze's view, all three of the foregoing functions took shape during the Frankish Empire, but with each function dominant during a successive period: the military function during feudalism's early period (through the end of the 12th century), the political function during feudalism's heyday (16-17th centuries), and the socio-economic function during feudalism's late period (through the 19th century). Hintze also took these three characteristics as the preconditions of feudalism in the absolute sense, i.e. in the sense of a system of state organization.

What distinguishes Hintze's approach is his emphasis also on historical influences. He said that feudalism in the absolute sense arises when world-historic events abruptly resulting in imperialism cause deflection away from the typical and normal linear development from tribe to state. With normal development, there is a linear progression from a tribal system to a rational and objective state system (polis state, republic), as illustrated by Greco-Roman society. But in the Frankish Empire, contact with the Roman Empire engendered imperialistic territorial expansion that led to an inexperienced administrative structure governing over a vast territory characterized by an undeveloped road system and still in the stage of an object economy. It is out of the difficulties presented by these latter circumstances that a feudal system arises. This is what happened in Japan, also. Contact with a different, more advanced civilization caused a shift to imperialism that led to distortion of the normal development pattern, causing Japan to descend into a difficult social situation resembling that of the West, and it was out of this situation that feudalism arose.

Besides Western Europe and Japan, Hintze included two other societies as examples of absolute feudalism: Russian feudalism, which arose as a byproduct of Byzantine imperialism; and Islamic feudalism, which came about as a result of the imperialism of Byzantium as well as Sassanid Persia. Hintze excludes the cases of China (Zhou) and Egypt (Sixth Dynasty and beyond), which are generally considered to be examples of feudalism, from his list of absolute feudal societies because he sees them only partially meeting his three static conditions and entirely lacking with respect to his dynamic conditions.

Strayer's View

Joseph R. Strayer (1904-1987), in an essay written jointly with Rushton Coulborn (1901-1968), espoused the view that feudalism is a method of government (*Feudalism in History*, 1956):

"Feudalism is primarily a method of government, not an economic or a social system, though it obviously modifies and is modified by the social and economic environment. It is a method of government in which the essential relation is not that between ruler and subject, nor state and citizen, but between lord and vassal. This means that the performance of political functions depends on personal agreements between a limited number of individuals, and that political authority is treated as a private possession."

(page 3)

Strayer further expressed the view that military functions are prominent in feudal societies, particularly in their early stages, and that these military traditions frequently remain to form specific ethical spirits: chivalry in the West, the "way of the samurai" (*bushidō*) in Japan, and the rites (*li*) of Zhou China. He also pointed out that there are strong tendencies for feudal societies to be ruled by nobility, to entertain a status-based system of hierarchy, and to embrace heredity of professional functions.

Elsewhere, in *Feudalism* (1965) Strayer repeatedly emphasized that feudalism is a system having to do with domination. "Feudalism," he wrote, "is a method of government, and a way of securing the forces necessary to preserve that method of government." (page 13) He further defined feudalism as a system encompassing the following three aspects:

> *1) Fragmentation of political power: Over much of Western Europe the county is the largest effective political unit, and in some places even the county is splintered into small, autonomous lordships.*
>
> *2) Private possession of political power: The political power can be divided among heirs, mortgaged, bought and sold.*
>
> *3) Vassalage and fief: Land and right to raise taxes are rendered in return for military service.*
>
> (pages 12-13)

Strayer opined that societies traditionally considered to be feudal demonstrate one or two of the foregoing three traits, whereas Japan exhibited most of them. Nevertheless he stated that it was in the West that feudalism first appeared and that it developed most completely.

Hall's View

John Whitney Hall (1916-1997), as noted earlier, in "Feudalism in Japan—A Reassessment" (1962) took up the definitions of feudalism that had been advanced by a number of others, extracted points common among them—the three sectors given below—and used those points as a basis for deriving his own definition.

> *1) Political sector: Lord-vassal complex in contrast with bureaucracy. Its essential element is not contract, but rather the personal nature of the association (symbolized by homage in Europe) and its military origin.*
> *2) Social sector: Hierarchy of social statuses in contrast with aristocratic slave-based societies and mobile modern societies.*
> *3) Economic sector: Landed, or locally self-sufficient economic bases distinguished from pastoral, commercial, or industrial.*

(pages 31-32)

Lenin's View

Vladimir Lenin (1970-1924), in *The Development of Capitalism in Russia* (1899), referred to feudalism from the perspective of an economic system as a "corvée economy." As its main features, he listed the following four characteristics:

1) The predominance of natural economy; the feudal estate had to constitute a self-sufficing, self-contained entity, in very slight contact with the outside world.
2) Such an economy required that the direct producer be allotted the means of production in general, and land in particular; moreover, that he be tied to the land.
3) Personal dependence of the peasant on the landlord.
4) Extremely low and stagnant condition of technique, for the conduct of husbandry was in the hands of small peasants, crushed by poverty and degraded by personal dependence and by ignorance.

(Hall, pages 29-30)

This view excludes the element of political domination stressed by Strayer and others and uses production and producer modes as its sole indicators. It is seen as a prototype of the general view of feudalism embraced by Marxist historians. To illustrate, *Weltgeschichte in Daten* [World History in Data], published in the former East Germany in 1965, describes the essence of feudalism as the combination of a low technical situation, land as the most important means of production, ownership of land by landlords and exploitation of peasants by landlords, and class struggles surrounding surplus produce. Another East German work, *Geschichte 6*, a history textbook for high school students published in 1984, portrays the essence of feudalism as peasants being the most important producers, exclusive land ownership by a feudal aristocracy that suppresses and exploits the peasantry, and the ideology of the ruler functioning as religion.

In East Germany and the other countries within the former Communist bloc, the division of history as a progression from slavery through feudalism to modern capitalism was applied equally to the whole world. According to the Communist view, the period of slavery encompassed the histories of Mesopotamia, Egypt, the Greco-Roman world, China and India in their entirety from the 4th millennium BCE through the 3rd century CE. The feudal period began between the 3rd and 7th centuries in the Mediterranean region, Middle East, India and China, and continued until the English Revolution in the 17th century; it was said to still exist even today in many areas of Asia and Africa.

Nagahara's View

Keiji Nagahara (1922-2004) also viewed feudalism primarily in terms of its social substructure. In an essay on feudal societies published in 1985, he addressed the two general concepts of feudalism—the legal historical view and the production mode theory (Marxist view)—and stated that the matter is not a case of one being correct and the other not. However, he said that the legal historical view, because it is concerned only with the collective form of the rulers, is inadequate for understanding social relationships in their entirety whereas the production mode theory is, to his thinking, the more comprehensive of the two because it simultaneously encompasses three issues: 1) peasants and method of farm operation (small family operation); 2) land ownership; and 3) power structure (power-based extortion by the landowner rulers of surplus produce in such forms as labor, produce, currency, etc.). He further added that since vassalage developed to an extent permeating throughout all society only in Western Europe and Japan, it is inappropriate to use the legal historical view as a theoretical framework of feudal societies within the historical contexts of various peoples and various states.

Scholars do not necessarily agree on this matter, however, and often they suggest the seigniorial system as a possible means toward bridging the gap. Nagahara, however, expressed the opinion that the legal historical view should be excluded. He argued that the seigniorial system, being a system in which, by dint of vassalage, the collective landowning class privately dominates the land and people, ultimately is fundamentally the same as the estate system—what European history scholars refer to as the fiefdom system—as an economic basis.

Elsewhere (Japanese-language version of *Encyclopaedia Britannica*, 1975 edition), though, Nagahara equated the production mode theory simply to the relationship between lord and peasant. Because the power structure enabling feudal domination of peasants by the lord is vassalage, he stated, the lord-peasant relationship and vassalage are in fact taken to be inseparable. Here, his contention approaches the legal historical view.

Indicators for Comparing Feudal Societies

The above completes my review of various definitions of feudalism offered to date. I will now proceed to seek an overview of feudalism by taking various elements — personal vassalage, enfeoffment, military service, fragmentation of political power, existence of a contract, status-based hierarchy, warrior culture, estate system and natural economy — as indicators for broadly examining and comparing societies that have conventionally been considered "feudal." The societies I will examine are those of Japan, Western Europe, China, Egypt, Byzantium, the Islamic world and Russia.

In proceeding, I will keep within the scope of the legal historical view. However, insofar as that view has traditionally focused on the progression of authority in the feudal system of Western Europe, I must exercise caution not to be swayed too far in that direction; at the same time, I must also be careful not to lay disproportionate emphasis on the feudalism of my own country, Japan. What constitutes "absolute" or "classic" feudalism will become evident from this process as it unfolds.

3

Japanese Feudalism*

In Japan, the formation and development of feudalism were closely related to the formation and development of private estates (*shōen*).

Japan's estate system continued over a period of 700 years, commencing with a system of reclamation of uncultivated lands in the mid-8th century, proceeding to a widespread system of "commendation-type" estates in the 10th and 11th centuries, peaking as a system in the 13th and 14th centuries, and dismantling in the late 15th century. Reclamation-type estates refer to estates of lands reclaimed, and consequently owned, by wealthy farmers, aristocrats, and Buddhist temples and Shinto shrines. These estates, directly managed by their owners, also came to incorporate lands purchased without legal justification from peasants in straits. Commendation-type estates refer to estates that were "commended," i.e. entrusted, by their owners to powerful central figures in the form of nominal ownership, in a quest to elude interference from state officials and other outsiders. These estates, over which the commending parties retained actual ownership, emerged nationwide, and as a system such estates were recognized under law in the 11th century.

---

*See Outline of Japanese History (p.@@)

Fundamentally, commendation-type estates comprised three parties: a proprietor, a manager and peasant cultivators. Proprietors were mostly court nobles and aristocrats residing in Kyoto and large temples and shrines. The estate manager was either a house member appointed by the proprietor, or the original owner who commended his lands to the proprietor. In the 11th century, this tripartite configuration came to be capped by a "protector"—a member of the imperial family or one of the regent houses—to whom the proprietor rendered nominal ownership. This estate system was a system of rights, known as *shiki*: namely, the right to hold an official post guaranteed under the authority of the state and the right to profit (from the land). The protector had the right to acquire from the proprietor part of the annual tribute he received; the proprietor, the right to collect annual tribute; the manager, the right to profit from managing the estate; and the cultivator, the right to till the land.

While the imperial family, court aristocracy and large religious institutions thus came to amass estates of enormous size, there continued to exist numerous public domains that traced their origins back to the centralization of power in the early 8th century. Records from the 12th and 13th centuries suggest that estates and public domains nationwide existed in equal measure, or perhaps in a ratio of 6:4. Gradually, however, the imperial family, aristocracy and religious institutions took private possession of the public domains and incorporated them into their estates while nominally retaining a state framework.

The warrior class emerged within this estate structure and developed parasitic to it. Warriors pre-existed already in the 9th and 10th centuries, but as estates became increasingly widespread, disputes with public domains and clashes between estates grew more frequent and farmers underwent growth within the estate framework, leading to a gradual increase in the number of warriors to deal with these developments. The warriors were organized around powerful upper-echelon peasants, and they were linked by their own ties of vassalage different from their relationship vis-à-vis the lord or state official. Early on they were scattered in isolated pockets and engaged in repeated skirmishes, but after the mid-10th century—i.e. around the middle of the Heian Era (794-1185)—they entered into ties of vassalage with powerful warrior leaders and formed into groups. This continued until one of the warrior leaders, Minamoto Yoritomo (1147-1199), founded the warrior government (*bakufu*) in Kamakura and was granted authority by the imperial court to appoint provincial constables (*shugo*) and place land stewards (*jitō*) on the estates and public domains, at which point the warrior bands metamorphosed from private vassalage-type organizations to public administrative and bureaucratic organizations.

The Kamakura *bakufu* was a unique power structure backed by powerful ruling families in the country's eastern quarters, its economic basis consisting of its directly controlled lands (its own estates) and regions under its rule (public domains). For each province, a powerful vassal known as a *gokenin* was appointed to serve as constable and granted military and policing rights. *Gokenin* were also appointed to serve as the land stewards, and these were granted authority to perform policing duties, levy annual tribute and labor service, manage their lands, and levy provisions. By holding military power of command extending nationwide, the warrior class came to form a state power structure in charge of government administration, in the same way that the court class centered on the emperor oversaw investiture and legislature and the Buddhist temples and Shinto shrines oversaw religious ceremonies.

The vassalage relationship of the Kamakura Period (1192-1333) was one in which formally a relationship was established after a would-be vassal secured an audience with the shogun (generalissimo); however, ties were also established simply by the would-be vassal reporting his name to Kamakura and the shogun in turn giving the vassal notification of his acceptance. This was a lifelong relationship based on mutual trust, and in the event that either party expired, the relationship ended. When a new shogun succeeded to the position, the relationship was renewed by holding audience with the vassal; when a new vassal supplanted one who had deceased, the shogun gave him a letter confirming guarantee of his right to rule over his landholdings.

The fief of the Kamakura era at times consisted of actual lands, but in most cases it equated to the *shiki*, i.e. right, to profit from the land. Of the enfeoffments carried out by Yoritomo, the most important was *jitō-shiki*, the right to be steward of a landholding. With this right, the enfeoffed had entitlement to levy a certain amount of provisions and extra harvest per given area of his appointed estate or public domain. The amount of land granted to the *jitō* varied from an entire village of considerable size to a small fraction of a modest village.

The foregoing vassalage relationships and practice of enfeoffment had already burgeoned during the Heian Era, but it was in the Kamakura Period, in tandem with the local fragmentation of political power in the form of the establishment of the *bakufu*, that they became widespread, giving rise to what is generally referred to as "Japanese feudalism." These three factors of feudalism—vassalage, fief, local fragmentation of political power—continued largely unchanged through to the end of the Muromachi Period (1333-1573). But whereas the political power framework was schematically unchanged, the balance of power shifted significantly, from the court centered on the emperor and the religious institutions to the warrior nobles, and the system of shared governmental administration came to be superseded by autocratic control by the warriors.

The warrior echelons had already been making inroads on the estates and public domains in the Kamakura Era in such forms as the appointment of land stewards, the delivery by the land steward of a fixed amount of harvest to the proprietor (*jitō-uke*) irrespective of the quality of the actual yield, and equal land ownership rights shared by the proprietor and the steward (*shitaji-chūbun*). Then with the transition into the Muromachi Era in the 14th century, along with the strengthening of the rights of the provincial constables, the estate system started breaking down as an outgrowth of new developments including the constables' provision of fixed amounts of harvest to proprietors and public offices (*shugo-uke*) and the granting by the Muromachi *bakufu* government of half the annual tributes from temple and shrine lands and public domains to the warriors (*hanzeihō*). As a result the warriors came to secure regional authority and, increasingly, control over whole areas. This trend became especially salient after the Onin War (1467-1477), when the *daimyō* feudal lords of the ensuing Warring States period rejected the estate system, enfeoffed the lands within their domains to their vassals, and, simultaneous with their increasing independence from the *bakufu*, gradually took direct and unified control over the people under their respective regional codes.

During the Edo Period (1603-1868), the *bakufu* controlled lands nationwide and the shogun distributed these lands to the *daimyō* in the form of fiefs. Each *daimyō* in principle granted land to his vassals and bestowed stipends on his underlings. The lord-vassal relationship between the shogun and the *daimyō* was established by receipt from the *daimyō* of a pledge to honor his official duties and observe ordinances. In the event of a change of shoguns, the new shogun had to issue a document renewing the *daimyō*'s control over his land and the *daimyō* was required to submit an oath signed in blood. In the event of a change in *daimyō*, the new *daimyō* had to submit his own pledge, again signed in blood. The same protocol was followed in establishing or renewing the vassalage relationship between each *daimyō* and his vassals. In return for the favors bestowed upon him by his lord, the vassal was obliged to perform military and labor service, as in the preceding era. But whereas military duty was the principal service of the earlier period when warfare was rife, during the Edo Era—a period of sustained peace—labor service became a heavy burden. The labor duties shouldered by the *daimyō* included: *sankin-kōtai*, a system of "alternate attendance" requiring that the *daimyō* reside in the capital (Edo, now Tokyo) at regular intervals; attend audiences with the shogun at regular intervals or whenever summoned; and undertake repair of temples, shrines, rivers, etc.

Within his own territory the *daimyō* had virtually unlimited authority; he oversaw administrative and judicial affairs and possessed the power to levy anything the land produced. The *bakufu*, however, monitored the *daimyō* under a system of "auditing officials." In the event of any uprising or revolt within a *daimyō*'s domain, the *bakufu* punished the parties responsible and imposed sanctions on the *daimyō* in such forms as reducing or transferring his domain; but normally the *bakufu*'s policy was not to interfere whatsoever in the *daimyō*'s internal affairs.

In contrast to earlier times when the class system was fluid, in the Edo Period the four social classes — warriors, farmers, artisans and merchants — became firmly fixed. Within warrior ranks there were innumerable grades of status. Even within the minor Sabae-han domain (50,000 *koku*), for example, there are said to have been 63 graded ranks between chief retainer (*karō*) and foot-soldier (*kachi*).

Western Feudalism

Next I will examine the feudalism of the West, focusing attention on the system of the land area that today encompasses France and Germany, where it originated.

The integration of vassalage and enfeoffment systems is first discernible in the West among the Franks of the Merovingian period, i.e. 6th to 7th centuries, particularly in the area lying between the Loire and Rhine rivers. In those days when a king expired, his territorial lands were customarily divided up among his surviving sons, creating a situation that engendered incessant disputes among the royal aristocracy, unending social unrest, discontinuation of tax levies and conscription by the state, and ultimately the division of administrative and judicial affairs among various local powers that separated off from the center. Within this turbulent environment, numerous freeborn individuals, in a quest to ensure their own safety, commended themselves and donated their lands to power regional families and pledged to till the soil and perform military service for them in exchange for protection. Earlier, in Gaul during the period when it was subservient to Rome there had existed a system of patronage known as *patrocinium*, encompassing protector and protected alike; and in Germanic society there had existed a unique system of "followers" (*Gefolgschaften*) who as hangers-on lived in the house of their tribal leader and did battles with provided horses and weapons. The system of vassals that emerged during the tumultuous Merovingian period is said to be based on both of these earlier systems.

Personal commendation during the Merovingian era did not always go hand in hand with the granting of a *beneficium*, i.e. fief; but after the transition to the Carolingian period in the 8th century, the vassalage system and the practice of enfeoffment merged into one coherent system. The Carolingian kings sought increased numbers of vassals in order to deal with internecine wars and launch battles to expand the royal territory, and in order to secure large numbers of warriors among such vassals the kings distributed lands to them along with the legal right to use and derive profit from them (usufruct). During the reign of Charlemagne this amalgamated system became even more pervasive, to the extent that even personages of high social standing—dukes, marquis, counts, bishops, abbots et al.—commended themselves to the king in return for benefices; and in tandem with this development, a status-based hierarchy took shape linking the upper and lower echelons of society in a chain of vassalage. The ceremony of commendation consisted of the vassal kneeling before his lord, placing his own clasped hands within those of the lord, and then standing, placing his hand on a Bible or holy relic, and reciting an oath of loyalty. The vassal was granted protection and a *beneficium* in exchange for his shouldering obligations to perform military service, escort service and procurement of funds. The *beneficium* chiefly was a grant of land (estate) accompanied by the right to profit off it, although at times it came with an official position (titled nobility, priestly office, castellan, estate officer, etc.). This arrangement ended when the vassal expired, and succession was renewed by the succeeding party commending and taking the oath of fidelity himself.

The empire unified under Charlemagne split into three during the reign of his successor, Ludvig. As the local families of power came to wield increasing influence, the situation descended into anarchy marked by frequent rebellions that gradually eroded all kingly authority. During the subsequent 9th and 10th centuries, Magyar, Saracen and Norman incursions devastated the empire, causing the central authority to lose its powers further. As a consequence, the local nobles had no alternative but to rely on their own resources to defend their territories, thereby raising their territorial focus to the point that they came to dominate their lands and peoples by dint of judicial, military and administrative powers cut off from the sovereignty of the king. Fragmentation of official powers gradually extended to the level of lesser nobles, and by the late 11th century castellans in France were able to maintain direct control and security over at best an area of some 20 kilometers from the castle site. By the 10th century nearly all free people possessing assets were incorporated into bonds of vassalage, and by the mid-11th century fiefs came to supplant lands owned outright (allod) and constitute the major portion of all land territory.

This period between the 10th and 12th centuries, when political fragmentation progressed to the point that vassalage and enfeoffment systems spread broadly and became the social norms, is thus referred to as feudalism's "classical" era. However, during this period the lord-vassal relationship as a whole moved in the direction of expanded rights accrued by the vassal; and succession and ownership of the fief, which had earlier been limited to a single generation, became common, giving rise to transfers and sales of such land properties. In addition, the desire of vassals to secure more land meshed with the landed lords' aspiration to secure increased service, and gradually multiple homages — one vassal serving multiple lords — came to be carried out broadly. One extreme recorded example is the case of a vassal in southwestern Germany who forged vassalic relationships with a remarkable 43 lords. Early in the 12th century, the landed fief came to be superseded by the money-fief, a practice that helped fuel this system of service to multiple lords. Under the new arrangement, the number of days served by each individual was reduced, the vassal could be exempted from military service through monetary payment, and money could be paid by farmers in place of labor service or rent in the form of land produce.

Subsequent to this trend toward "realization" of feudalism in the classical era, in the latter half of the 13th century feudalism lost its role as an essential element of Western European society. The human element within the lord-vassal relationship became secondary, and both commendation and the oath of fidelity typically became perfunctory procedures for obtaining the right to hold a fief. Under the monetary economy that developed during the 12th century, society demanded a new structure different from feudalism. Urban-based commercialism broke down regional barriers and sought to expand as far as possible. Urban citizens only required their own mutual assistance, and their morals were completely different from the code of vassals. In addition, a mercenary system based on monetary wages was more convenient than knighthood, and the emergence of firearms stripped knights of their *raison d'être*. As education spread among urban echelons and the number of people able to read and write thereby increased, there arose professional administrators having the ability to calculate accurately and judges possessing knowledge of the law. Hiring such individuals as bureaucrats and entrusting administrative, financial and judicial matters to them was more efficient than domination via complicated lord-vassal relationships.

In this manner, Western feudalism gradually broke down; yet even after vassalage effectively disappeared, in many regions domination of estates by lords continued into the 17th, 18th and 19th centuries even as the shift proceeded to a monetary economy. Because being a lord was a social honor and was accompanied by substantial rights to profit, alongside the nobility there gradually arose an increasing number of lords drawn from the urban populations.

Thus ends my overview of Western feudalism as it was found in France and, somewhat later, in Germany.

A Comparison of Japanese and Western Feudalism

When comparing the feudal systems of Japan and the West, in both one can easily recognize elements including domination by warrior families, personal vassalage, fiefs, a status-based hierarchy, local fragmentation of public power, a system of estates and a natural economy. Other noteworthy points shared in common are the formation of a unique culture founded on the warrior's view of life and death and code of conduct and, in the later phases, the growth of a monetary economy and salient development of urban populations centered on merchants and artisans.

Where the systems of Japan and the West differ, I offer, is in the following three ways: their respective economic bases, changes in the form of their respective systems, and relative strength or weakness of their pledged ties of allegiance.

Concerning their economic bases, Japanese feudalism is marked by a strong parasitic nature. The economic base, the estate system, was a land system born from the ancient centralized state system (*ritsuryō-sei*) of the 8-9th centuries. The lords of these lands were the imperial family, the court nobles and the religious institutions. In the Kamakura Period, the newly emerging warrior class first became dependent upon the estates through the establishment of the *jitō* land stewards; and subsequently they made further inroads in the forms of the aforementioned *jitō-uke* (provision of a fixed amount of harvest to the proprietor) and *shitaji-chūbun* (equal ownership of land rights by the proprietor and the steward). In the Muromachi Era, this economic base was whittled down further by *shugo-uke* (constables' provision of fixed amounts of harvest to proprietors and public offices) and *hanzeihō* (granting by the *bakufu* of half the annual tributes from temple and shrine lands and public domains to the warriors). In this way, feudalism maintained its existence and continued to grow. This possession of estates based on ancient authority sustained itself even as the Warring States Era *daimyō* exclusively dominated whole lands in the late Muromachi years, only to finally disappear with the land survey carried out by Toyotomi Hideyoshi (1537-1598).

In Western feudalism one does not find this type of parasitic dependency on other social systems, and estates were either possessed outright by the feudal nobility itself or held by them. Compared to Japan, their economic base was simple in form. This difference in their respective economic bases is closely intermeshed with the difference in the purity of their respective systems of political domination. In Japan, the remnants of the ancient *ritsuryō* system of centralized government that preceded feudalism, which was a system operated by the emperor and court aristocracy, sustained itself over a prolonged period by dominating and subsuming feudalism, even as it gradually weakened in strength. By contrast, in the West the ancient wielders of authority—kings and churches, for example—were brought into the framework of feudalism early on, with the result that the state system was purely feudal.

The second point of difference—change in the form of feudalism—has to do with the fact that in the case of Japan feudalism underwent a change during the Edo period from the earlier fragmented allocation of public powers at the local level to centralization of such powers. Although this is similar to the concentration of power under the French feudal monarchy after the 13th century, the French monarchs joined with urban forces, availed of their monetary economy to undermine the domination of domains by the nobles, enlarged their crown lands, and gradually expanded bureaucratic administrative and judicial structures in their lands to national scope, whereas in the case of Japan the Tokugawa shogunate came to dominate the entire country at a single stroke and power came to be concentrated by entrusting the administration and judicature of the various regions to local authorities based on vassalage relationships. What this form—an overlay of centralization upon the feudal (*daimyō*) domain system of the preceding Warring States period—more closely resembles is the feudal system of England after the Norman Conquest. In the case of England, what had been a conglomeration of regional forces rallying under systems of vassalage and enfeoffment as on the Continent, was transformed by the Duke of Normandy, William the Conqueror, into a strictly ordered centralized feudal system. After the Conquest (ca. 1027-1087), the Duke gathered all his lords around and made them pledge their loyalty and offer up their land holdings to him personally, whereupon he distributed them anew. He also investigated the lands throughout the country, drew up a land ledger, and used it as a standard for tax collection and conscription. This is identical to the measures and policies implemented by Toyotomi Hideyoshi and Tokugawa Ieyasu (1543-1616).

The third difference between Japanese and Western feudalism is in the degree of strength of the contractual nature of the lord-vassal relationship. In Japan the relationship was by and large a bilateral contract, with the lord providing a fief to his vassal in exchange for the latter's loyalty and service. But rather than being a legally binding relationship involving rights and obligations, the lord-vassal relationship in Japan was heavily dependent upon feelings of mutual trust at the personal level, to the extent that a Japanese proverb went: "The relationship between parent and offspring exists only during one generation; the relationship between man and wife spans two generations; and the relationship between lord and vassal spans three generations." In particular stress was laid on the total devotion of the vassal toward his master and ruler, and serving two masters was deemed an act of immorality. By contrast, the lord-vassal relationship of the West was heavily oriented toward legal rights and obligations and strongly contractual in nature, with service and favor offered in equal measures on a reciprocal basis. Given the weakness of the human element involved in such relationships, serving multiple lords was a natural outcome, and already by the 9th century there appeared cases of service to multiple rulers under a plurality of contracts. This arrangement gradually became commonplace, and before long serving a single lord came to be considered exceptional and "heroic."

Tetsuro Watsuji (1889-1960), in his *Nihon rinri shisōshi* [History of Japanese Ethical Thought, 1952], asserts, citing numerous sources, that under the lord-vassal relationship of Japan's feudal warriors it became customary for the closely shared existence of the lord and his vassals to induce both sides in the relationship to stifle personal interests and to put the other party's interests first, with the lord setting aside his own interests and even staking his own life for the sake of his vassals and the vassals devoting themselves to such a lord with all the greater emotion and passion. Watsuji further states that this customary behavior by warriors centered on unmitigated devotion and realized selflessness existed not only among the warriors themselves but permeated deeply into the court nobility and peasant farmer class as well. By contrast Saburo Ienaga (1913-2002), in his *Nihon dōtoku shisōshi* [History of Japanese Moral

A Comparative Study of Feudalism

Thought, 1954], contends, also citing quite a number of examples in the literature, that "without the slightest room for doubt" the thoughts and actions of warriors emanated from the utilitarian and self-serving aims of seeking to maintain and expand their personal territory and to ensure the prosperity of their own future generations. Ienaga avers that the warriors' loyalty and service to their lord were always predicated on offering such loyalty and service in exchange for rewards of these kinds.

This clash of opinions between Watsuji and Ienaga surrounding the ethics of the lord-vassal relationship, whether that relationship was based on a sense of sincerity or on a sense of calculated self-interest, has often garnered the attention of Japanese historians, and the various parties to the debate have each passed judgment favoring one side or the other. But if the question at hand here is defining the "average" warrior characteristic of the entire period in which warriors flourished in Japan—a period spanning seven or eight centuries—then, given how changes occur within the flow of time and individual warriors all have different natures, I would suggest that building an argument leaning toward one side or the other based on evidence drawn from the literature is quite unlikely to yield any convincing conclusion; what is needed to resolve the issue is to shift perspective and examine the matter from diverse angles. One such perspective is to make a comparison with the West, where service to multiple lords based on what today would be called multiple "contracts" became widespread early on. Another new perspective offering promise would be comparing issues addressed in the literature of the warrior age in Japan with those central to the literature of other cultures, in the following manner.

A look at the medieval literature of Europe shows that the epic poetry forming its mainstream existed in two types: heroic poetry and court poetry. Of the two, heroic poems do in part deal with allegiance to one's lord, as illustrated by France's *La Chanson de Roland* (The Song of Roland) and Germany's *Nibelungenlied* (The Song of the Nibelungs). In many instances, however, the main themes that make up the central storyline are man's innate dark and sordid thoughts: ingratitude, betrayal, cunning, revenge, etc. The court poetry falls into categories such as tales of King Arthur, stories about Tristan and legends relating to the Holy Grail, and all of these deal with themes unrelated to the ethics of vassalage: supernatural adventures, magical gardens, loving service to one's lady, etc. Also, within the realm of lyric poetry it is love poems about devotion to married ladies of the court that form the mainstream.

When one compares this medieval European literature with the medieval literature of Japan, which centers on tales of war and historical events, the two differ clearly in where they respectively lay stress and in tone; and within this comparative perspective also, the answer emerges that in Japan the ethics of affection and loyalty between lord and vassal strongly defined the nature of medieval society. While (a) the answer can point exclusively neither to loyalty nor self-interests alone, (b) the two are inevitably interrelated, and (c) a comprehensive judgment must subsequently be rendered by taking into consideration other perspectives, the response based at least on the two perspectives just described must be said to lean in favor of Watsuji. Max Weber defined the feudalism of the Merovingian period as *Gefolgschaft* (*trustis*), whose distinguishing characteristic was a strong human element founded on loyalty and devotion to the lord, in contrast with the bilateral-contract type feudalism of medieval Europe at its heyday. He also used the identical term, *Gefolgschaft*, to characterize the feudalism of Japan as a whole. His view falls in line with my own interpretation.

Chinese Feudalism

Chinese feudalism refers primarily to the system of the Zhou Dynasty.

In the 11th century BCE, Zhou Wuwang overthrew the Yin (Shang) Dynasty and set up a capital at Zongzhou, awarding fiefs to his blood relations and loyal retainers. His successor, Zhou Chengwang, eliminated residual elements of the Yin and constructed a second capital at Chenzhou (Luoyi), using it as his main base for ruling over the east. Chengwang carried out a second round of enfeoffment, this time taking fifty-some states belonging to the House of Zhou, setting them among the several hundred previously existing feudal states and using them as his key strongholds from which to rule. The state at this time was a spontaneously engendered small dominion consisting of farmlands and a few small villages centered on a walled capital city (*dayi*), and whereas Yin had been one such state that had brought others under its political umbrella in the form of a confederation, Zhou's new system was an artificially devised rearrangement of its Yin precursor. The imperial orders bestowed upon the nobles in the ceremony of enfeoffment recorded the amount or size of their fief: the amount of farmland being granted, size of its central city, number of surrounding villages, number of carts and horses, and number of armed troops. Later these details were inscribed on bronze vessels, enabling their passage down to posterity. In exchange for their fief, the lords were obliged to provide annual tribute, labor service and military service. The feudal lords were divided into ranks of peerage — the Chinese equivalents of dukes, marquises, counts, viscounts, barons — and each was served by a group of retainers of noble status: the dukes by *qing dafu* (=*shang dafu*, grand or upper ministers), marquises by *xia dafu* (lower ministers), counts by *shang shi* (upper servicemen), viscounts by *zhong shi* (ordinary servicemen), and barons by *xia shi* (lower servicemen). The lords bestowed lands upon these retainers in amounts befitting their respective status.

Both the relationship between the House of Zhou and the feudal lords and the relationship between the lords and their ministers and servicemen were governed by the principle of blood lineage, and the performance of political governance was integrated with religious ceremony worshipping commonly shared ancestors. The imperial house was like the main family, with the feudal lords corresponding to branch families; the lords sought clan solidarity through marriage, and the whole was one family, a patriarchal state system in which the ruler embraced constituent members with the benevolent love of a father. Within each state also, a system of rule similar in nature was seen, i.e. the feudal lord ruled over the clan community as patriarch.

Within 200 years after the Zhou Dynasty's founding, the cohesion of this patriarchal religious community weakened, the authority of the House of Zhou atrophied, and the power of the feudal lords alone flourished. Within the states also, the *dafu* ministers came to supplant the lords in wielding real power, capable *shi* servicemen were assigned positions on a contract basis without concern for blood relationships, and they came to participate in government administration. The absence of a power of authority gave rise to numerous internal dissensions within the states along with contests to grab landholdings, and it also became common for the lords to lead armies to do battle with other states, bringing them down and incorporating them into their own. In this manner China headed into the Spring and Autumn and Warring States periods, times of major upheaval.

A comparison of this Chinese feudal system with the feudalism of Japan and the West reveals many points in common: systems of private vassalage and enfeoffment, a status-based hierarchy, local fragmentation of public power, a natural economy, etc. Where the Chinese system differs is that whereas the feudal systems of Japan and the West were both dominated by the warrior class, in the Western Zhou period the court and aristocracy, in the Spring and Autumn and Warring States periods the scholar-bureaucrats, held sway at the center. Also, while both Japanese and Western feudalism were preceded by centralized bureaucratic states marked by formidable royal power, the corresponding Western Zhou state, though it was characterized by strong royal power, was a decentralized state fundamentally no different from the state system of the Spring and Autumn and Warring States periods.

Egyptian Feudalism

Feudalism in the context of ancient Egypt generally refers to the period of six to seven hundred years commencing with the Fifth Dynasty (2500-2350 BCE) of

A Comparative Study of Feudalism

the late Old Kingdom and ending with the Twelfth Dynasty (1990-1800 BCE) of the Middle Kingdom.

The royal power of the pharaohs of the Old Kingdom (2700-2200 BCE) reached its zenith in the Fourth Dynasty, as symbolized by the great pyramids of Khufu, Khafre and Menkaure. During the Fifth Dynasty their power gradually weakened, and the nobles who had been granted vast landholdings by the royal household gathered strength and secured a monopoly on the important posts within the central government; governors too settled in and solidified their local power bases, thus giving rise to the feudal trait of fragmented power. Whereas through the Fifth Dynasty such nobles were buried alongside the royal tombs at Memphis, the capital, rather than in the regions to which they had been assigned, and their final resting places were modestly marked by titles such as "judge and governor," in the Sixth Dynasty the nobles constructed magnificent tombs for themselves in the cities they governed, and their burial grounds proudly proclaimed their titles: friend of the pharaoh, head of the city, administrative officer, governor, etc. Along with the monopolization and succession of official positions by the aristocratic minority and the emergence of an independent regional nobility, another new force to be reckoned with were the temples that had been granted vast landholdings from the royal household and grown wealthy under the protection of special privileges of immunity. The authority of the pharaohs held on by a thread through the reign of Pepi II at the end of the Sixth Dynasty, but after his demise any remnant of power evaporated and the nation split asunder, descending into anarchy and ushering in a period of upheaval. This period—known as the First Intermediate Period (2200-2050 BCE)—was marked by incessant warfare among minor local powers as the kingdom languished during the Seventh and Eighth Dynasties under a succession of numerous short-lived pharaohs for whom little historical evidence exists.

Eventually, the Heracleopolitan kings subdued this chaos and came to the fore, creating the Ninth and Tenth Dynasties. They were subsequently overthrown by Theban kings supported by the nobles of Upper Egypt, bringing in the Eleventh Dynasty. Egypt was once again unified, this time with its capital at Thebes, marking the start of the Middle Kingdom period (2050-1800 BCE). The local nobles maintained their earlier power, however, ruling over their domains as minor monarchs and continuing to use their own unofficial reign names. Then in the Twelfth Dynasty, administrative reforms were vigorously implemented, the aristocratic forces were driven out, reign names were unified, and royal power finally emerged from entrenched stagnation and came to loom loftily over the nobility. However, this was not a restoration of the absolute, autocratic, divine prerogative of pharaohs as in the Old Kingdom, but only the supremacy of royal power lacking a stable basis and heavily dependent on the powers of the aristocracy and temples.

After the two hundred years of the Middle Kingdom, Egypt again slipped into a period of chaos known as the Second Intermediate Period, when foreigners known as the Hyksos came to rule directly over northern and central Egypt and indirectly, through the kings of Thebes, over southern Egypt. This domination by outsiders continued for one hundred and fifty years until the arrival of the New Kingdom (1580-1100 BCE).

From the situation of Egypt just described various factors can be recognized as in the cases of Japan and the West: local fragmentation of public power, an estate system and a natural economy. But insofar as personal vassalage and enfeoffment systems are concerned, the possibility of their existence is strong but the actual situation is unclear. It is also unknown whether warriors formed classes and whether this was a period imbued with a unique ethos.

Byzantine Feudalism

Byzantine feudalism is usually spoken of in connection with the *pronoia* system. *Pronoia* refers to the system of benefices carried out as the official policy of the Komnenos Dynasty of the 11th and 12th centuries, a system under which the emperor granted estates—known as *pronoiai*—to aristocrat lords in exchange for their provision of military service.

Earlier the Byzantine Empire had had a system of "themes." The theme system originated in the 7th century when, during an era of turmoil stemming from incursions by Persians, Arabs and Slavs, among others, military units (themes) throughout the empire developed quasi-independent local administrations. Once a crisis had passed, such units were placed under the control of the central government and administration of the themes was entrusted to the military commanders. The soldiers, in lieu of monetary payment, were given plots of land, and in times of peace they, together with their families, worked their plots as farmers. The system was thus one characterized by military districts and soldier-farmers. In the 10th and 11th centuries, with the development of a commodity economy there developed a class of lords (aristocrats by lineage) possessing vast territories incorporating large numbers of farmers and amalgamated lands, ushering in the dismantling of the theme system. As the military commanders became ruler aristocrats, an increasing number of soldier-farmers evaded military service through monetary payments, returned or sold their landholdings, or simply fled. In the mid-11th century these powerful families with vast land properties supported the Komnenos Dynasty and, availing of the emperor's expansive marriage policy, became part of the imperial family, whereupon they achieved rank within the hierarchy topped by the emperor and their lands were recognized and appended. As a consequence, conscription of soldier-farmers became difficult, necessitating the introduction of a system of mercenary soldiers, thereby putting a drain on government coffers, and it was as a result of this that the *pronoia* system was adopted as a countermeasure.

Initially *pronoiai* were granted, along with the right to collect taxes, to the smaller lords belonging to the military aristocracy in exchange for taking to the battlefield together with mounted troops of a number proportionate to the size of the estate. At this stage the grant was limited to a single generation; but before long the system came to be used by the imperial family and upper aristocracy and it shifted in the direction of succession, thus providing a means enabling the large aristocrat landholders to obtain even larger lands. The result was a flood of feudal rights within the empire during the first half of the 12th century. From precisely this time through to the end of that century, Western lords and military men who had participated in the Crusades began settling in the empire in large numbers, bringing with them Western feudalism, which was very similar. As this imported form of feudalism spread, it gave rise to a feudal society indistinguishable from that of Europe, and this system continued until the Ottoman Turks invaded and destroyed it during the 14th century.

Nearly all discussions dealing with Byzantine feudalism typically focus on the *pronoia* system and make passing mention of the preceding theme system. However, the theme system is of no real pertinence since it was a simple system of farmer soldiers, and even the *pronoia* system differed considerably from the feudal systems we examined earlier. Of the various elements seen in the feudal systems of Japan, China and Western Europe, the *pronoia* system did involve enfeoffment, an estate system and the superiority of a military nobility; but it lacked the elements of personal vassalage and local fragmentation of public power. The *pronoia* system was, in short, a system of conscription, and for a number of reasons — the fact that the right of land ownership, even after estates came to be passed on by succession, was under the discretion of the emperor; the fact that centralized control of administrative, financial and judicial matters continued; and the fact that the system did not include any personally formed lord-vassal relationships — it can be construed as a system attendant to a centralized bureaucracy. This is perhaps why the *pronoia* system immediately gives the impression of being different from the feudalism of Japan or Europe.

Islamic Feudalism

Turning next to the Islamic world, here too we find politico-military systems very similar to the *pronoia* system: systems commonly referred to as "Islamic feudalism."

One example is the timar system of Turkey during the Ottoman era (late 13th — early 20th c.). Under the *timar* system, military administrators known as *beylerbey* and *sanjakbey* were assigned to the empire's various states and provinces; together with their commanding officers (*spahi*) and cavalrymen (*suipahi*) they took charge of administrative and military affairs, and in lieu of monetary payment estates of various sizes were granted to them in accordance with their respective ranks: *khass* in the case of a commander, *ziamet* for officers, and *timar* for members of the cavalry. All estates were public lands, however, and what was granted was not the right to land ownership but rather the right to collect taxes. The sultan blocked the *beylerbey* and *sanjakbey* from assuming rulership over their respective territories by shifting them from one assigned area to another in short intervals; and to keep in check the *timar*, which accounted for nearly all the estates, the sultan imposed legally intricate rules enabling centralized control and, through measures such as collectivization of the fiefs, made it difficult for landlord-farmer relationships to form. In essence the *timar* system, like the *pronoia* system, was thus an administrative system linked to the centralized power system for the purpose of securing soldiers in times of emergency. The *timar* system began breaking down when the central government started losing its influence at the regional level in the 17th century, i.e. in the latter half of the Ottoman period. The *timar* and *ziamet* estates lost their status as fiefs and became objects for trading, leading to the ownership of large land properties by powerful local families.

The same kind of system existed in Egypt during the Mamluk sultanate. The Mamluk sultanate was an Islamic state whose sphere of influence centered on Egypt but also included Palestine, Syria and Lebanon. With its capital at Cairo, the sultanate continued for 250 years, from the mid-13th century until early in the 16th century, when it was vanquished by and incorporated into Ottoman Turkey. The sultanate's ruling class was made up of Byzantines during the 13th through 15th centuries and Caucasians during the 15th and 16th centuries. Like Ottoman Turkey, a military form of government was adopted and administrative and military affairs were entrusted to officers assigned to states throughout the sultanate territory: upper-class nobles known as emirs serving in positions as commanders of divisions, regiments, squadrons and companies, and mounted aristocrats known as *al-halqa* serving as platoon commanders. The emirs were granted the right to collect taxes from between one and ten villages, dependent on their rank, and the *al-halqa* were granted corresponding rights relating to a portion of a village. As in the case of Ottoman Turkey, the central government monitored these fiefs closely. Initially the upper-class nobility managed the lands of the lower-class aristocracy, but later all lands belonged directly to the sultan and an array of measures were implemented to prevent all nobility from forging close ties with their regions: these included frequent changing of their assigned locations, dispersion of fiefs and collective holding of fiefs. This system of centralized control, strict though it was, began weakening in the 15th century, however. Tax collection rights came to be traded, and the fiefs lost their inherent status and became the private property of powerful regional families.

The reason the Ottoman and Mamluk organizations resembled each other so closely is said to be because they are both based on the *iqta* system of military government that came to be carried out broadly within the Islamic world starting from the 10th century. In the case of the Ottoman system, the influence of the preceding Byzantine *pronoia* system is also suggested. The relationship between the *iqta* and *pronoia* systems is unclear.

Russian Feudalism

Three points must be considered when discussing feudalism in Russia: the partition system, *pomest'e* system and Western feudalism.

Partition was the state system in place when the Russian principalities were isolated under Mongol domination, i.e. between the 13th and 15th centuries. Earlier, in the 9th century Scandinavians had passed into Russia and set up a state centered on Kiev, assigning magistrates to govern the local states. Commerce flourished, primarily through trade with Byzantium, enabling the formation of a wealthy merchant class among the native Slavs. In the 11th century, in place of local rule by magistrates a measure was implemented whereby the royalty came to govern the states in rotating succession. Before long, however, the princes ceased such movements from state to state and took to settling in a particular state, ushering in private ownership of land by noble service officers (Germanic military men) and local aristocrats (Slavic merchants). In tandem with the commencement of Mongol domination in the 13th century, the principalities became isolated, and simultaneously fractionalization into numerous partitive lands occurred as a result of increased numbers of family members. The lords of these partitive lands possessed administrative and judicial authority as well as their own state army. The noble service officers served under them, but their service was not based on a contract of loyalty or on the granting of a fief; while retaining their own hereditary lands, they were able to change their service locations to places irrelevant to the location of their hereditary land. Through this period farmers too were, like the nobility, free to move at their will; there was no serfdom tying them to the land. This system of partition is the first point to consider when discussing Russian feudalism.

In the 15th century Russia finally extricated itself from Mongol domination and Muscovy, which played a major role in winning liberation, rapidly gathered in strength and became the central force in Russia. The Muscovy principality broke down the partition system, concentrated power at the center, and confiscated and nationalized the lands (farming villages) of the hereditary nobles in large volumes. It then took these lands and, in the form of *pomest'e* (fiefs), distributed them to noble service officers, court servants and farmers, with a lifetime limitation period, in exchange for military service. In the case of the nobility, they were obligated to go to battle accompanied by fully armed followers in numbers proportionate to the area of the land they were granted. In addition, the nobility were prohibited from freedom of movement and the freedom of the farmers was also limited, being forbidden from leaving the land beyond a set number of years. Gradually, as the *pomest'e* owners applied increasing pressure, the farmers became tied to the land.

From the latter half of the 15th century the *pomest'e* system accrued complex mechanisms and was widely implemented, and in the second half of the 16th century the total land area of the *pomest'e* fiefs came to exceed that of the hereditary lands by a wide margin. Furthermore, the fact that such fiefs were tied to military service gave rise to the notion that military service was a requisite of land ownership in general. Conventional hereditary land ownership became limited to cases in which military service could be carried out, and when such service could not be performed, measures were taken to confiscate such lands. Thus, the nature of hereditary land ownership came to involve obligations and conditions close to the nature of fief ownership. At the same time, fief ownership too gradually approached hereditary land ownership in nature—for example, when the period of service drew to a close, normally 20 percent of the fief was granted to the individual involved as hereditary land, and the remaining 80 percent was open for cash purchase. In the latter half of the 17th century, exchanges and commercial trading of fiefs became common and was recognized under law. Finally, under laws promulgated by Peter the Great and Empress Anna in the early 18th century, fiefs ultimately were merged with hereditary land as the property of their owner.

The system most generally referred to when discussing Russian feudalism is this *pomest'e* system. The system is similar to both the Byzantine *pronoia* and Islamic *iqta* systems, and its founding is normally attributed to the functioning of the *pronoia* system, in particular because Russia was traditionally under the powerful influence of Byzantine culture, especially during the 15th and 16th centuries when the *pomest'e* system was inaugurated.

The third point to consider when discussing Russian feudalism—Western feudalism—is the simple issue of imitation and assimilation. In western Russia, Western feudalism took hold progressively beginning with those regions closest to Europe. Galicia, which was in the Russian west, participated in the Third Crusade (late 12th c.), and Prince

Vladimir paid homage to Byzantium's Manuel Komnenos. Also, it can be ascertained from 15th century lists of nobles serving in Muscovy that a considerable number of Germanic were included among Russia's central aristocracy, partly attributable to inroads by the Teutonic Knights into the area east of the Baltic Sea commencing in the 13th century. Furthermore, indirectly attributable in large share is the fact that Byzantium, on which Russia as a whole was highly dependent both politically and culturally, became a feudal society after the 13th century through its assimilation into Europe.

4

Selection of Major Elements

The foregoing completes my overview of the social systems traditionally referred to as "feudalism"—those of Japan, Europe, China, Egypt, Byzantium, the Islamic world and Russia—based on general criteria including such elements as a system of private vassalage, an enfeoffment system, local fragmentation of public power, military service, a status-based hierarchy system, contracts, and an estate system.

Next, from among these elements I will select the major ones and construct an "ideal" feudalism type; but first, it is necessary to clarify which of the two types of feudalism I examined earlier is "true" feudalism. One type is the feudalism of Japan, Europe and China, where the term refers to a state system in which public power is fragmented locally. The other type is that of Byzantium, the Islamic world and Russia, where feudalism is a substructure within a state system in which public power is concentrated at the center. In the former type, power to rule is shared by a monarch and numerous members of a nobility; in the latter, ruling authority is the exclusive prerogative of a single monarch. As to which of the two is "true" feudalism, this should become self-evident based on (a) the fact that the concept of feudalism derives from the type found in Japan, Europe and China, while the type extant in Byzantium, the Islamic world and Russia is clearly an application of the concept; (b) the fact that the concept of feudalism is generally understood to indicate the form of a society or state in its entirety, and not to indicate an administrative system; and (c) the fact that feudalism is generally understood to indicate status-based domination, and not absolute domination.

If the feudalism of Japan, Europe and China contains the kernel of the concept in its essence, then the following can be said concerning the "ideal" feudalism type we are seeking.

First, the foremost constituent factor is that feudalism is a state system. Feudalism does not indicate a designated organization within a society, nor a transitory system within a society; it is an ordered system of society as a whole, or of the state as a whole, that continues on a sustained basis—in other words, a system of state.

Second, local fragmentation of public power ranks as a major constituent factor. State systems come in two opposing formats: one in which public power is concentrated at the center, and the other in which such powers are fragmented locally. Feudalism belongs to the latter type: i.e., feudalism is a concept diametrically opposite to a system of centralized power. This fact is aptly indicated in the terminology of China, where traditionally the concept of feudalism (*fengjianzhi*) has continuously been used in a sense opposite that of *junxianzhi*, the centrally controlled commandery-district system.

At the same time, the local power-holders who possess their respective shares of ruling authority are personages of a hereditary noble class with ranks and official positions: i.e., weight should be accorded to the factor known generally as a status-based hierarchy or status-based domination. Local fragmentation of public power and status-based hierarchy can be lumped together and be expressed as the fragmentation of public power to local lords.

The third important factor is the presence of personal vassalage and enfeoffment systems that function as mechanisms enabling the fragmentation of public power to the local lords. Personal vassalage, in contrast to a system of bureaucracy, refers to relationships formed on the basis of individual character, sealed by personal contracts. Enfeoffment expresses the material aspect of such contracts.

Among the five factors I have just named—a state system, local fragmentation of public power, status-based hierarchy, personal vassalage and a system of enfeoffment—all except the first are factors that frequently appeared in the definitions of feudalism offered up by the various experts discussed earlier. Among them, the most prevalent cases defined feudalism using only two elements: personal vassalage and enfeoffment systems. Ganshof, who described feudalism simply as "*institutions féodo-vassaliques,*" is a prime example. However, using these two factors alone does not make for an accurate definition, for such a definition would also encompass organizations such as the mafia and yakuza. Only when the element of local fragmentation of public power is added does the inherent meaning of feudalism take on strength and breadth; furthermore, only when the elements of a status-based hierarchy and a state system are added can feudalism be differentiated from all other political systems and social situations.

Into the term "status-based hierarchy" I wish also to infuse the sense of status-based domination. Status-based domination is, as we saw earlier, a term used by Max Weber to indicate a stage of development in which an aristocratic minority shares ruling authority: a transitional stage between patriarchal domination by a single absolute monarch and legal domination ruled by reason. This is a historically accurate analysis of feudalism and it has significant weight as a way to distinguish feudalism from other social forms.

Furthermore, in my view the most indispensable element indicative of the framework of feudalism is the system of state—even though this element is not included among the pointers just used in investigating the various societies under consideration, and even though among the views offered by the cited sources it appears only in the definition of Hintze and is emphasized only by Yōzō Horigome as the order of the system of state. Without the element of a system of state, it would be impossible to differentiate feudalism from the rampant state of confusion of local forces that repeatedly appeared throughout the course of world history.

A note of caution is needed when discussing local fragmentation of public power. This is because the term "local fragmentation of public power" also encompasses local government in modern centralized bureaucratic states.

In my view, local fragmentation of public power comes in three types:

(a) local government within a centralized system; public powers are divided qualitatively and by area of specialization;

(b) cases where central authority lacks force and public power as a whole is locally fragmented; public power is simply divided quantitatively;

(c) cases as described in (b) in which there is a mantle of centralized authority; quantitative division of public power is maintained.

Among these, (a) expresses the local administrative systems that constitute the centralized system recognizable in both the autocratic, patrimonial bureaucratic states of ancient times and the democratic, rational bureaucratic states of modern times. (b) includes not only the periods referred to as feudal in Japan, Europe and China (Spring and Autumn and Warring States periods), but also the situations of periods generally said to be marked by social upheaval. (c) is a system that retains the situation described in (b) but also has a framework of centralized authority resting over it; examples are the *bakufu/daimyō* feudal system of Tokugawa Japan, the feudal system of England after the Norman Conquest in the 11th century, and the system of China during the Western Zhou period. Local fragmentation of public power, the point at issue in discussing feudalism, clearly applies in the cases of (b) and (c) but not (a).

The "ideal" type of feudalism is comprised of the foregoing five factors, but even within the definitions based on only two or three of those factors, in many instances the remaining factors are present as underlying premises. Within the "*institutions féodo-vassaliques*" of Ganshof cited above, for example, a further perusal of his works reveals that local fragmentation of public power and the state system figure in as prerequisites. The way they are abbreviated, however, would seem to be the cause for the confusion that has existed in the concept of feudalism until now. When such omissions occur repeatedly, the omitted factors gradually are forgotten and attention focuses only on those factors that appear on the surface, and feudalism comes to be thought of, for example, only in the context of a system of land grants and military service. When this happens, the system of farmer-soldiers also qualifies as feudalism; and indeed, Max Weber counted the system of farmer-soldiers as an example of "feudalism in a broad sense."

In addition, explanations and definitions of feudalism normally treat its various constituent factors in the manner of a list of individual and equal components, and this listing method would seem to be one cause behind the inconsistency of the feudalism concept. Following this method, the *pronoia* system of Byzantium, *iqta* system of the Islamic world, and the *pomest'e* system of Russia all appear to incorporate my factors: they all more or less qualify as systems of state; they involve local fragmentation of public power (of the kind described in (a)); they have what appear to be enfeoffment systems; and, because they have a privileged military class, they are status-based hierarchies. Since the only factor they lack is a personal vassalage system, it would not be strange in the least for these to be considered feudal systems. This is all the more so since they also involve the factors of a natural economy and an estate system, which are likewise accorded equal treatment.

The five factors I offer up are not arranged equally in the horizontal direction but rather are in a relationship of subordinated chained links in the vertical direction. The system of state is a large abstract framework; local fragmentation of public power (as opposed to centralized authority) and status-based domination (as opposed to patriarchal or legal domination) are its substance; and personal vassalage and enfeoffment are its specific configurations. Enfeoffment too, by virtue of its being a material aspect of personal vassalage, is linked vertically, and for this reason not even one of the five factors can be abbreviated. The farmer-soldier system is already eliminated in the first stage, and the *pronoia* and other systems are eliminated in the second stage.

I take the foregoing five factors as the primary constituent elements of feudalism's "ideal" type, and take the others as its secondary constituent elements. The military aspect need not be taken up in particular since military service is an element included within personal vassalage, and the fact that the ruling class is the military nobility is not likely to be a determining factor of feudalism. Estate systems and a natural economy exist at all times and in all regions, and in feudal societies they merely provide a backdrop. The culture of chivalry, which has its own sentiments and ethics and gave birth to distinctive arts, does not appear to be so important as a political element, and arriving at a clear definition is not easy. Contracts, in view of their inclusion within personal vassalage, for that reason inherently do not need to be taken up; however, because they have often been stressed before, I would like to discuss this point later.

France's Feudal Monarchy

The foregoing completes my task of putting together the "ideal" concept of feudalism. Here, I would like to discuss a debate that exists concerning the French feudal monarchy, in a desire to clarify my view further.

Generally, feudal monarchy is seen as a phenomenon marking the denouement of French feudalism. The French monarchs sought to challenge the feudal lords and expand their sovereign authority by joining forces with the urban-dwelling powers that arose in tandem with the development of a commodity economy. They also expanded lands under their direct rule by seizing fiefs on the grounds of infidelity to the feudal lord or the absence of an heir to the fief, adopted money-based fiefs rather than land-based fiefs, and imposed lord-vassal relationships with sweeping thoroughness. In addition, they further concentrated their personal power by progressively replacing the feudal armies, which were unstable and inefficient, with a system of mercenary soldiers. The French monarchs also established state bureaucrats known as *bailli* (bailiwick) and *sénéchal* (seneschal) and absorbed into their unified state authority the judicial, administrative, financial and military powers that until that time had been the prerogatives of the local nobility. As the monarch's lands expanded, so too did the numbers of *bailli* and *sénéchal* officials. Initially itinerant, these bureaucrats came to stay permanently on their appointed lands starting in the 14th century. This trend toward unified state rule was subsequently maintained and strengthened, leading to absolute monarchy from the 16th century onward. This series of events constitutes a denial of local fragmentation of public power, and as such can be taken as a departure from feudalism.

The view has been expressed, however, that with feudal monarchy feudalism reached its zenith.

In *Yōroppa chūsei sekai no kōzō* [The Structure of Medieval Europe, 1976] Yōzō Horigome (1913-1975) presents the following view. Earlier, he says, when monarchic power was weak, authority was vested in the allods and in the church system extant outside the boundaries of feudalism, a situation that gave birth to formidable complexities in fief-granting relationships. Then in this later period, against the backdrop of the development of an exchange economy monarchic authority grew, monetary power gave rise to a system of civil servants, and relationships involving granting of fiefs centered on the monarch. Feudalism, Horigome suggests, inherently is not contradictory or in opposition to the state or monarchic authority; in its very emergence there already exists an underlying trend toward the formation of a state order centered on the monarch. Feudalism, he continues, appeared to incessantly harbor the risk of anarchy, while medieval society in reality never gave a hint of any risk of anarchy. Unlike the conventional view that lays stress only on feudalism's aspect of being in conflict with the state or monarchic authority, Horigome claims that if one focuses on the meaning and role of feudalism in the formation of the political order of the state or monarchic power, then this offers ample reason to consider the feudal monarchy period that led to the realization of such a political order as feudalism's zenith.

Horigome's view conflicts with the established view of the academic world, which places the zenith of European feudalism in the 11th and 12th centuries and sees the French feudal monarchy of the 13th century as a transition period leading to the dismantling of feudalism. His view is also unconvincing in that, broadly speaking, Horigome perhaps treats too lightly the element of political disintegration in feudalism.

Terushirō Sera (1917-1989) refuted Horigome's theory in the following way. Nearly until the 12th century, he argued, extremely narrow limits were imposed on expansion of the de facto base of monarchic power, and it was precisely this circumstance that necessitated a feudal power (state) structure. As such, when such limitations were rescinded, feudalism completed its inherent role and effectively shifted, inevitably, into a phase of its own dismantling. The zenith of feudalism in the 13th century—which is when the limits on monarchic power expansion were removed via the processes of the monetary economy's emergence and the breakdown of the villication system—was thus none other than the process of feudalism's own self-conquest.

In Sera's view it is the feebleness of monarchic power that constitutes the very reason for feudalism's existence—a view that is easy to understand. From the perspective of the "ideal" type of feudalism, the following can be said.

An examination of Horigome's view demonstrates that his thinking on feudalism is based chiefly on the three elements of vassalage, enfeoffment and state order. I too emphasize these three factors, but to consider feudalism as being based solely on those factors naturally implies that the feudal monarchy period, when all of these factors were fully in evidence, constitutes the zenith of feudalism. However, when the factor of fragmentation of public power to local lords is added in, this view immediately collapses since the feudal monarchy period was a time when public power became increasingly centralized. Accordingly, we must accept the conventional view.

As a political order, feudalism in essence was a local fragmentation of public power, not a centralization of power. If one keeps this most crucial point in mind, then regardless of how much stress is placed on the factor of this political order, the only types of system that would conceivably qualify as the zenith of feudalism would at most be the *bakufu/daimyō* feudal system of the Tokugawa period or the centralized feudalism of England.

Contracts

The general view of feudalism, especially that embraced by European scholars, stresses the bilateral contract entered in the lord-vassal relationship, and there is an overall trend to evaluate more highly those feudal systems in which contractual ties were strong. But contracts setting down rights and obligations are of the same dimension as personal relationships based on affection and trust insofar as they both indicate how ties connect people, and thus for contractual relationships to be evaluated more highly than personal relationships they must clearly be the more essential to the feudal system. The only person whose explanation, to my knowledge, rested between the two was Max Weber, and the general thinking on feudalism appears to draw heavily on his view.

Weber, as described earlier, suggested three forms of domination: charismatic, traditional and legal-rational. He further differentiated two types of traditional domination: one a patriarchal structure of despotic domination by a single ruler, and the other a status-based structure of domination by a small number of nobles who share their power with an overlord. Weber saw feudalism as representative of this latter type. He further characterized the former type as arbitrary and the latter as contractual. He said that in a feudal system vassals are completely free and independent: i.e., they submit to a bilateral contract and not to a patriarchal ruler, and the nature of this relationship becomes increasing stronger over time.

"Feudalism is a status-based patrimonialism, a marginal case that contrasts with patriarchal patrimonialism."
"The essence of feudalism is status consciousness, and it increasingly perfects this very characteristic."

Furthermore, Weber extends this association to legal-rational (modern capitalistic) domination and charismatic domination, and he offered the following description of the position of feudalism within all types of domination:

"As the household with its patriarchal domestic communism evolves, in the age of the capitalist bourgeoisie, into the associated enterprise based on contract and specified individual rights, so the large patrimonial estate leads to the equally contractual allegiance of the feudatory relationship in the age of knightly militarism. The personal duty of fe-

alty has here been isolated from household loyalties, and on its basis a cosmos of rights and duties has come into being, just as the purely material relationships were isolated when the enterprise developed."

As this demonstrates, Weber's various types of domination do not merely indicate stereotype differences; they can also be said to point out phases of historical development together with phases of logical development. Personal relationships during this process can be understood as a transition from religious passion (piety) in the form of submissive devotion and faith, through loyal allegiance or sincere human feelings, to a calculable and purely material relationship—in short, strength of passion and contractual strength increase and decrease in inverse proportion. Accordingly, the view becomes possible that because feudalism is in a position close to a modern, civil, contractual society after having been a patriarchal society, the greater are its degrees of freedom and of contractual strength; a shift is required in personal ties from blood-based relationships to material relationships; and the stronger such material ties, the more "genuine" is the feudal system. Weber, in fact, appears to have thought along these lines. This assessment can be made based on the way, while consistently stressing a vassalic relationship founded on sincerity, as a requisite of genuine feudalism he states that people must be in a mutually free contractual relationship as independent beings (which is the opposite of a relationship founded on sincerity) and not in a patrimonial, subservient relationship; also, among all feudal relationships Weber stressed "free" feudalism, and he especially accorded foremost treatment to the feudatory free feudalism of Europe, which was strongly contractual, and to the prebendal free feudalism of the Oriental countries, which was completely devoid of any relationships based on sincerity.

While I acknowledge the position Weber accords to feudalism among his various forms of domination, to my understanding his classification scheme goes no further than determining the relative spiritual state of feudalism as a social type and describing feudalism as having relatively higher levels of freedom and contractual strength than the patriarchal domination that preceded it; his scheme does not suggest that the higher those levels, the closer feudalism approaches being "genuine" in form. If, instead, the genuineness of feudalism is sought in the strength of the contracts binding one free individual to another, then—to take the argument to its extreme—one would have to conclude that the society most feudal in nature is our modern civil society. Of course, Weber is talking about an "extreme case" within the framework of the traditional domination type and his issue is thus limited to the level of contractual strength within that framework. But even so, following this argument the period of "true" feudalism in the

West would be the period starting in the 13th century—which is generally seen as the period of feudalism's dismantling.

To my understanding, the existence of various levels of emotional ties—in other words, the existence of various levels of intellectual ties—within the vassalic relationships of feudalism is merely indicative of feudalism's diversity, and not indicative of differences in levels of genuineness or maturity. Both Japanese and Merovingian feudalism—which, being based on affection and allegiance, are what Weber referred to as *Gefolgschaft* types of feudalism and thus are remote from genuine feudalism—and Western feudalism—which incorporates freedom and contracts and is hailed as true feudalism—are feudal systems in equal measure: one is not "above" the other. Whether the system leans toward emotions or toward intellect depends on the time frame or on the character of the people involved. During the early stage of a period of status-based domination, there is a strong element of emotion residual from the preceding period of patriarchal domination; and as the era of status-based domination approaches its denouement, the intellectual element of the subsequent period of legal domination increases. As the differences in the inborn nature of the particular people in this scheme—whether they are more emotional or intellectual, more humane or materialistic, more antiquated or modern—add in, actual differences in the contracts of respective periods emerge. Japanese feudalism looked during the Warring States Period as if it would abandon the ties of affection that bound vassals to their lords, but in the Edo Period such ties actually strengthened; and Western feudalism, conversely, was rational and developed the notion of a right of resistance during its early phase, and began shifting to a system of allegiance to multiple lords already in the 9th century—a trend that underwent no changes thereafter.

Although the relative strength and level of permeation of personal vassalage serve as yardsticks for measuring the genuineness of a feudal system, and the bilateral contracts that gave rise to personal vassalage are a special feature that distinguishes feudalism from the patriarchal system that preceded it, the nature of personal vassalage (i.e., its contractual strength) is no more than a secondary matter of no consequence insofar as the feudal system is concerned. As such, I believe the matter of contracts should be subsumed within personal vassalage, which I listed as a fundamental constituent element of feudalism, and should be deleted from the mainstream of our discussion.

Conclusion

In this chapter my task was to probe the inherent meaning of the concept of feudalism. In other words, what I sought to do was not to create a new "ideal"

A Comparative Study of Feudalism

feudalism type but rather to find the underlying ideal type that already exists. What I did was to distinguish two types within the societies that have generally been viewed as manifestations of feudalism; I viewed one group (the feudalism of Japan, Europe and China) as the legitimate line, and at the base of these I ascertained five important factors linked vertically. I then used this set of five factors as feudalism's ideal type. From a fairly early period, the meaning of the feudalism concept became confused, specific examples became entangled, and this confusion and entanglement were used as excuses for the incessant evident moves attempting to converge the concept into one individual manifestation, that of European feudalism. As a set the five factors are expected to bring order to the foregoing confusion and bring a halt to such moves toward a specific example of feudalism.

Some may voice the opinion that having only three societies correspond to the ideal type is narrowing the definition too far. However, as each of the three societies is an independent and self-reliant form of feudalism, these three examples may be said to suffice to qualify feudalism as a universal concept. Moreover, since the application range of this ideal type is broad—as demonstrated by the facts that (a) a similar society existed in Egypt, (b) feudalism approaching this ideal type is often indicated in reference to Peru, and (c) there are people who see feudalism in this sense in the polis (city-state) system of Greece—I believe this ideal type is useful as a means of historical analysis.

CHAPTER TWO

The Formation of Feudalism

Although an enormous number of studies have examined how individual feudal systems, those of Japan and Europe included, came into existence, to date virtually the only one that has dealt with the formation of feudalism in general from the perspective of world history is the aforementioned study by Otto Hintze published more than 80 years ago: *Wesen und Verbreitung des Feudalismus* [Essence and Diffusion of Feudalism], dating from 1929. One other study on the topic is Rushton Coulborn's *A Comparative Study of Feudalism*; but as Coulborn's thinking is quite rough and arbitrary, here I will take up Hintze's study alone.

Hintze's study is short, only some 30 pages in the

original, yet to this day it has consistently been accorded the highest level of respect as a classic masterpiece in the area of feudal studies, especially comparative feudalism. In his work Hintze addresses two points: the essential nature of feudality and the rise of feudal systems as intertwined with that feudality. By placing the definition (i.e., essence) of feudalism I reached in the preceding chapter in contention against that expounded by Hintze, I aim to make my argument all the more solid. Furthermore, because I have my own perspective on how feudal systems came into being, I aim, while pointing out and picking apart the contradictions and problems in Hintze's theory, to indicate a completely different type of interpretation.

Three Factors of Feudalism

To begin, I offer the following overview of Hintze's main points. For his "ideal" type of feudalism Hintze looked to the Frankish Empire—which he says was the source of the word "*Feudalismus*"—and the states that succeeded it. He said this feudalism had the following three functional factors:
1) Vassalage and enfeoffment of professional warriors (military function)
2) Manorial system of peasant farmers serving lords (socio-economic function)
3) Fragmentation of public power among local lords

(political function).

Under the Frankish Empire, systems of vassalage and enfeoffment became the norm, with professional warriors becoming vassals to a lord via personal contracts and performing military service in exchange for receiving fiefs. This eventuated as a consequence of (a) the fact that even as the empire expanded its territory, an object economy prevailed and roads and transport means remained undeveloped, and especially (b) the pressing political urgency to deal with the Saracen threat. This is feudalism's military factor. Meanwhile free peasants commended themselves and donated their lands to powerful religious and secular leaders, resulting in a gradual strengthening of land subordination and turning the peasants into serfs, with estate owners guaranteed unearned income from ground rent. This is the socioeconomic factor. Moreover, the position of counts, who were the appointed governors under the Frankish Empire, became increasingly hereditary and tied to specific lands; the public domains, through acquisition of the right to conduct court trials and rights of immunity with respect to taxation and inspection, became private possessions; and as a result public power became fragmented among local forces, inviting the creation of separate states. This is feudalism's political factor.

These three factors seen in the Frankish Empire and its successive states, insofar as they constitute a state system in which they function under mutual restraint, correspond to feudalism in the true sense of the word. When only one or two of the three are in evidence or when they are recognized merely as burgeoning, the situation at hand doesn't qualify as feudalism at all. In ancient Egypt during the Sixth Dynasty, for example, although increasing independence of local lords and broad-based subordination of farmer peasants are in evidence, there isn't so much as a trace of a system of grants to vassals. In ancient China under the Zhou Dynasty, lands were distributed in the state's interests, especially to protect its borders, and grants were made based on the recipient's status, with attention paid to ancestor worship but going no further. There were no warrior aristocrats based on military service and contracts of allegiance, peasants generally remained small farmers over prolonged periods, and no estate system strongly subordinate in nature developed. The feudalism seen in the Great Mongol-Islamic Empire was only a burgeoning form of political feudalism in which public power was wielded as the personal prerogative of powerful local landlords; it was only a fragment of socio-economic feudalism marked by an estate economy of landlords and subordinate farmers; and in fact it did not consolidate to the level of feudalism as a state system. Other than the case of Europe, the only examples of feudalism in the true sense, where it consolidated to the level of a state system, are the feudal systems seen in Russia (*pomest'e*), the Islamic world (*iqta*) and Japan.

Among these three, it is in Japan especially that the foregoing three factors are fully present and demonstrate a surprising level of similarity with Western feudalism. The *pomest'e* system of Russia and the *iqta* system of the Arab-Ottoman Empire are state systems in which estates having subordinate farmers were widespread and administrative and military rights were wielded by warrior aristocrats who lived off unearned ground rents. Although they lacked the element of a vassalage system, they can be counted among examples of full-fledged feudalism.

Genuine Feudalism: A Product of the Constellation of World History

In addition, in each of these three systems the backdrop to feudalism, remarkably, is an intermingling, significant within world history, of cultures sharing aspects with Western feudalism. Rather than being the product of internal national development, feudalism arises from the constellation of world history that appears only within larger cultural spheres.

In the case of the Frankish Empire, because it came in contact with the civilized society of the Roman Empire during the process of its transition from a system of loosely organized tribes to a strongly consolidated state order, its normal linear development was impeded and, suddenly and without intervention, it was compelled to leap over numerous stages and trace a hasty path to imperialism via expansion of territory through successive conquests. In the process, on one hand the difficulty arose of governing, with only immature means at its disposal, an expansive territory in which roads and transport means were undeveloped and which lacked rational and institution-like organizations. Meanwhile on the other hand, the psychological difficulty arose of attempting to adapt to the universal challenges presented by Roman civilization. The means of coping with these dual difficulties was feudalism.

Normal linear development refers to a tribe directly developing into a state. A classic example is the Greco-Roman Empire, where tribal societies grew into city-states having rational and objective institutions without going the roundabout route of becoming a despotic empire along the way. In the new European world also, the nations of Eastern Europe and Scandinavia were impacted by Western feudalism but, because they had no contact with imperialism, fundamentally they were able to form states without feudalism. By contrast, Egypt and China, though also examples of states that had no contact with imperialism, experienced a semblance of feudalism simply because, unlike Greece and other nations where state formation was limited to a small area, they each unified myriad small states and inflated into a larger state, and dominating their expansive areas came to exceed the power of the state.

Contrastingly, the feudal systems of Russia, the Islam-

The Formation of Feudalism

ic world and Japan are of the same type as Western feudalism; and they became feudal systems because in their respective transitions from tribe to state they were each dragged down the path of imperialism by the example set by imperialism in the context of world history.

In Russia the example of imperialism was set by the Byzantine Empire. Starting in the 15th century the princes of Moscow, roused by Byzantium's imperialist doctrine, adopted a policy of territorial expansion and cultivated groups of professional soldiers by giving them land and residents for their fiefs. The princes then dispatched these warrior groups on distant military missions and used them for colonization purposes. This *pomest'e* system, unlike the partition system that preceded it, had both military and socio-economic factors, and is therefore worthy of being called "genuine" feudalism. However, it lacked a system of vassalage and, more than chivalric honor or fidelity, its purpose was de facto military service. Also, the political factor of feudalism (local fragmentation of public power) gradually vanished as the Duchy of Moscow centralized its authority and went totally out of existence after the reign of Ivan the Terrible.

In the case of the Islamic peoples, the imperialist example was set by the Eastern Roman (Byzantine) Empire and the Sassanian Empire of Persia. When the Arabs expanded their land conquests with religious zeal, they left the existing systems and Byzantine and Persian bureaucracies intact, and adopted the *iqta* system to form the core of their warriors. The *iqta* system, similar to the enfeoffment system of the Franks, granted estates with an imposed limitation of a single generation, and the lord of the fief exercised broad political power over his subservient people. Like the *pomest'e* system, however, the *iqta* system lacked a system of vassalage.

In the case of Japan, the evolution to an imperialistic state philosophy did not occur directly through conquest-based expansion, but rather was triggered in reaction against expansion through comprehensive cultural acceptance. Through the introduction of the government system of China's Tang Dynasty (618-907) under the Taika Reforms of 645 CE, Japan emerged from a patriarchal clan state to a centralistic bureaucratic state. The ideology that initiated this state formation was Confucian doctrine. This autocratic state collapsed in the late Heian Period (794-1185), and in place of allotted rice lands private estates known as *shōen* became prevalent. Based on the *shōen*, a warrior class emerged, and among the warriors systems of vassalage and enfeoffment came into being. With these systems at its core, the resulting social system, while metamorphosing in various ways, continued until the second half of the 19th century. This system not only contained the three factors of Western feudalism in their complete forms, but also exhibited elements in common with the West such as chivalrous sentiments and the ethics of unconditional devotion.

As the foregoing demonstrates, although the imperialism of Europe, the Islamic world and Russia differs from the imperialism of Japan—the former directly linked to expansion through conquest or colonization and the latter taking the form of a comprehensive cultural acceptance of a governmental system and ideology—in both instances feudalism appeared not as one stage within the development of the peoples involved, but as a reaction to external world-historical developments, i.e., as the result of the adaptation of new peoples to superlative old forms of culture and civilization. Centralized state administration within the preceding empires was possible only in the presence of a highly advanced transport system and a well-regulated tax system. Without either of those systems and with only imperialist philosophy and expansive territory, territorial domination would have to rely on a principle of individual patrimonial domination of fragmented regions. It is here that feudalism—in the complete sense—emerges.

Problems with Hintze's View

Hintze analyzed the essence of feudalism and offered his interpretation of its formation in the manner described above. Although his writings are rich in vitality and have the power to pull the reader in, there are problems in the way Hintze assembles the overall structure of his argument itself, and the conclusions he draws leave us with substantial doubts.

He begins his argument by taking Western feudalism as feudalism's model, and he equates the distinguishing features of Western feudalism to the genuine nature of feudalism as a whole. Specifically, Hintze wrote that feudalism's "ideal" type must be based on the feudalism of the Frankish Empire, which was the source of the term, and on the feudal systems of the states that succeeded it. This same contention is made by Marc Bloch and others. However, given the existence of cases in which the term for the feudal system has no relation to the Western term—as in the cases of Japan and China—this way of thinking is unacceptable. Furthermore, even in reference to regions in which Hintze claims that the feudal system took the name from the Western term, to attach special importance to a word because it marks a first appearance is to give preference to mere words over reality—and to do so is unreasonable. Alternately, no matter what other reason besides the origin of the term one might cite, the fact that any number of similar examples exist and one of those is indeed extremely similar to Western feudalism, it is clearly inappropriate to take the specific case of Western feudalism as the norm or classic case. To insist on saying so even while admitting this fact is nothing but a manifestation of Western centralism. Regrettably this sophistry is a trademark not only of Hintze, but rather is something engaged in all too commonly. An ideal type must be sought in line with realities, apart from linguistic concepts. Inherently it should be kept at a distance from specific cases of any kind; common distinguishing characteristics must be extracted based on numerous specific examples; and the various characteristics should be aligned according to their order of importance, to assemble the ideal type.

The transgression committed by Hintze at the outset of his argument does not, however, have an adverse impact on his subsequent inquiry, and it does not erode his argument to any significant extent. The three factors that comprise his ideal type of feudalism — the military factor (lords and professional warriors bound by fidelity), the socio-economic factor (relationship between manorial lords and peasant farmers) and the political factor (local fragmentation of public power) — may be drawn from Western feudalism, but ultimately they are in the main appropriate as a depiction of a universal concept of feudalism.

Where a problem emerges is in Hintze's citing of societies which he claims conform to his ideal type of feudalism.

Hintze states that the foregoing three factors are indispensable conditions for feudalism in complete form, and he says that if only one or two factors are in evidence — or exist only in a germinant state — then the society in question cannot be called feudal. But alongside Western and Japanese feudalism, where all three factors are found, Hintze also counts among complete feudal systems the *pomest'e* system of Russia and the *iqta* system of the Islamic world, both of which can be said to lack the military factor (they have no vassalage system). Meanwhile Hintze excludes from feudal systems the systems of Egypt (Sixth Dynasty and beyond) and China (Zhou)—which are often cited as examples of feudal systems—on the grounds that the Egyptian case had no military factor by virtue of its having no trace of a vassalage system and the Chinese case lacked both military and economic factors because it gave rise to no warrior aristocracy and failed to have fully developed estates. He describes the Egyptian and Chinese systems as examples of burgeoning or fragmentary feudalism.

Reason for Hintze's Differentiation

What is the source of Hintze's contradiction, his dichotomy of assessments?

In Japan, Russia and the Islamic world, Hintze recognizes a world-historical constellation in which tribes were prevented from undergoing natural development to a state via involvement with other cultures similar to that of the West, i.e., through the example set by a more advanced civilization, and instead were forced in the direction of imperialism. Hintze says a situation of this kind served as the backdrop that gave birth to feudalism. In my view, however, such a situation was more than simply a backdrop: it was a constituent factor of the ideal type and wielded greater power than his three cited factors. As such, I conjecture that Hintze made little issue of the lack of the original three factors and used only this one factor as his basis for considering whether a society was a "complete" form of feudalism or only a "burgeoning" or "fragmentary" one.

As for what this all means, Hintze appears to single out and suggest one formative condition shared by all complete feudal systems, but in truth he defines complete feudalism using examples that conform with the formative condition he has set down from the start. As a result it is only natural that he arrives at the "correct" answer to his question as to what constitutes the formative condition of complete feudalism. Given how this section dealing with feudalism's formation is the centerpiece of his treatise outlining his notion of feudalism, his zeal is understandable. However, feudalism's ideal type should be defined only based on its innate essence; its formative condition, being its backdrop, surely must be treated separately.

When treated separately, however, does Hintze's formative condition — an "imperialistic leaning" — still apply? In the cases of Western and Japanese feudalism, it does. But if its application to only those two societies is deemed inadequate and the scope of application is extended to other societies, a problem arises in the discrepancy between the cases of the West and Japan — which gave rise to "complete" feudalism in the sense that they encompassed all three factors—and the cases of Russia and the Islamic world—which produced "incomplete" feudalism. A further problem arises in the cases of Egypt and China, which both gave rise to incomplete feudalism despite the absence of Hintze's formative condition. As a common factor, therefore, this formative condition undeniably lacks sufficient strength.

Feudalism's Essence: Another View

Because, as we have seen, feudalism is a phenomenon produced not by a single society but by multiple societies, defining the concept must be based not on one example of a special society but rather on the examples of multiple societies. To reach a definition, first a general judgment of the conventional range of the word's meaning must be made; next, one must focus on multiple societies that have traditionally been referred to as "feudal systems"; and finally, major factors based on those examples must be determined anew.

This is the process I undertook in the preceding chapter. I found that societies traditionally considered to be feudal divide qualitatively into two groups: those of Japan, Europe, China and Egypt on the one hand, and those of Byzantium, the Islamic world and Russia on the other. Because the former group can be said to be the "legitimate" one, from the members constituting this group I extracted a chain of factors: a state system, local fragmentation of public power, a status-based hierarchy system (status-based domination), personal vassalage and an enfeoffment system. I then used these to represent the ideal type of feudalism. Obviously, in this instance the feudal systems of Japan, Europe and China qualify as "complete." In the case of Egypt, no systems of personal vassalage or enfeoffment can be recognized. In the case of Russia, the partition system, although at times referred to as feudalism, also has no systems of personal vassalage or enfeoffment; but the system can be said to be nearer to feudalism than the *pomest'e* system. The *pomest'e* system and the Islamic *iqta* system, both cited by Hintze as examples of complete feudalism, belong to a different grouping. As their state systems are centralized, and thus antipodal to feudalism, for this reason it is altogether inappropriate to call these systems feudalism.

Comparative History of Civilizations

Insofar as the formation of feudal systems is concerned, the impact of imperialist influence from other societies suggested by Hintze no longer stands as a cause common to those societies we acknowledge as examples of feudalism—Japan, Europe and China—nor to the society of Egypt. As Hintze himself states, in the case of China we can find no influence whatsoever from an external political regime. In the case of Egypt, a Sumerian influence is conceivable, but the general view rejects this notion. Here, I will attempt to resolve this matter from a different perspective.

Earlier (in my book titled *Tagen bunmei shikan* [A Comparative History of Civilizations], 1991), I identified a group of "special" civilizations among the many to have existed historically. My groupings are similar to those proposed by the exponents of comparative history of civilizations who appeared primarily after the mid-19th century—historians such as Heinrich Rückert, Nikolay Danilevsky, Kurt Breysig, Oswald Spengler, Arnold Toynbee and Philip Bagby—who classified civilizations into culture-historical, high culture, independent and major types. However, whereas the criteria those historians used to set their classifications weighed heavily toward elements dependent on the subjective view of the classifier—criteria including cultural borrowing, originality, influence, great art-style and philosophy system—I excluded such subjective views and arbitrary interventions and relied only on objective elements to serve as the criteria for judging what I define as special civilizations. My criteria are actually only single in number: the passage of the civilization through four phases of history each spanning four to five hundred years. The four phases exist in two varieties: type A, which is a progression from a tribal confederation to a unified state, to a period of disturbance, to a world empire; and type

The Formation of Feudalism

B, which is a progression from parallel tribal states to parallel city-states, to a period of disturbance, to a world empire. Based on the foregoing criteria, I identified eight special civilizations classified into two groups: type A consisting of the civilizations of Egypt, China, Japan, Europe and Peru; and type B consisting of the Sumerian, Greco-Roman and Indian civilizations.

Classifying civilizations into different groups this way is typically greeted with criticism: the critic charging that the classifier determined in advance which civilizations to classify, selected facts suiting his purpose from among the limitless store of historical facts available, and then merely created rules and criteria tailored to fit his chosen facts. My response to such criticism would be that those who cast such aspersions have never actually attempted to make such classifications themselves. Virtually all histories of nations and regions are compiled without regard for a historical view of rules; but when a comparison of the histories of the many civilized societies on our planet is actually undertaken, it should become readily obvious that civilizations correspond to each other in various similar aspects. Such correspondences may be agreement with respect to changes in political system, changes in spiritual circumstances, or length of existence — patterns that are all objective and inherently leave no room for subjective opinion. In the case of my predecessors, subjective and arbitrary elements invariably have been factored in as well, so that unfortunately this aspect lies hidden beneath the surface. Inherently, however, the basis of a comparative history of civilizations is an unmistakably clear sense of commonality recognizable between civilizations; rules and criteria are merely the means of defining such points in common.

For each of the eight civilizations I cited above, I undertook a detailed examination of the four phases spanning four to five centuries. I also pointed out a number of concomitant phenomena such as technological progress, flourishing of cities, commercial and industrial development, decline in royal authority, rising power of the masses, and intellectual growth. I named civilizations of this kind "α-group civilizations." I also took up a number of civilizations that do not belong to that group, gave an overview of their histories, and noted those points in which they differ from the civilizations in the α-group, a process that was useful for underscoring the α-group's group integrity.

The foregoing are the main points of my approach to a comparative history of civilizations. Next, I will present how, based on this viewpoint, I interpret the formation of feudal systems.

I wish to note here that in recent years, in lieu of the term " α-group civilizations" which I used previously, I now refer to this group of civilizations as "major civilizations" (e.g., in my *Hachi-daibunmei* [Eight Major Civilizations], 2008). The latter term is more familiar to readers, and I will use this term in the discussions that follow.

New Interpretation of the Formation of Feudal Systems

The first point I wish to draw attention to is that the four societies whose feudal systems we have recognized as "genuine"—i.e., Japan, Europe, China and Egypt—all belong to type A major civilizations. In the process of deriving our ideal type of feudalism, there was no connection whatsoever with a comparative history of civilizations; conversely also, in our discussions of a comparative history of civilizations, α-group civilizations (major civilizations), type A civilizations, etc., no consideration pertaining to feudalism was involved at all. The fact that the conclusions reached in two independent discussions having no relation to one another coincided so precisely this way leads us to contend that the two justify and strengthen each other's argument. In line with the problems being addressed here, can we not say that the feudal systems of Japan, Europe, China and Egypt form a group, and with respect to various matters such as their formation and decline this grouping invites an approach from the perspective of the major civilizations?

Using the example of Japan, simply stated the historical progression of type A major civilizations is as follows.

The first phase of Japanese civilization encompasses: its birth in tandem with the formation of the Yamato court of Queen Himiko, a development recorded in Chinese annals as the first lengthy record pertaining to Japan; a period characterized by the existence of distinct structures known as tumuli (burial mounds); and a period in which, politically, a tribal confederation was ruled by a single reigning monarch whose power gradually expanded and strengthened. This phase continued for four and a half or five centuries (200/250-700 CE).

Starting from the mid-7th century, the political and cultural systems of China were then introduced into Japan, a state system on par with those of its neighboring nations was put in place, and with the enactment of the Taiho Code (701 CE) a powerful centralized and unified state was legally completed in which all powers were concentrated in a divine king known as *tennō*, i.e., emperor. This marked the formation of a state governed by laws, and politically and socially Japanese civilization proceeded to maintain this systemic framework of a law-based state (*ritsuryō* state) throughout the subsequent 1,200 years. However, this centralized system did not continue forever: from the Heian era onward actual political power passed into the hands of the aristocracy, "ownership" of all lands and the entire populace by the emperor broke down, and the aristocracy, temples and shrines, and powerful local families increasingly came into possession of large landed estates, with the result

The Formation of Feudalism

that dominating authority effectively became progressively fragmented and divided among these parties. This is the second phase, that of a "unified state" enduring for four and a half centuries (700-1150 CE).

Next, confrontations and rivalries among the various power forces intensified and military conflicts developed. After war broke out between the Minamoto and Taira clans (1150-1185), disturbances were triggered that embroiled the entire nation—including power struggles between the imperial court and the ruling Hojo clan, war against the invading Mongols, internecine struggles between the Northern and Southern Dynasties, widespread peasant riots, the Onin War, and the ensuing Warring States Period—and these continued until the formation of the Tokugawa regime. This is the period that came to constitute the core of Japanese feudalism; and although it lacked stability and was characterized by incessant unrest, and despite its being a feudal system—which on the surface might suggest a stagnant regionalism—progress was seen in material aspects: for example, increased production capability enabled by progress in farming techniques, commercial and industrial development, the flourishing of urban centers, and the spread of both monetary and commodity economies. In addition, creativity unique to Japan blossomed brilliantly in aspects of spiritual culture: for example, the formation of Japanese Buddhism; war-inspired literature; developments in historical thought; performing arts including Noh theater and comic farce (*kyōgen*); the tea ceremony; *ikebana* flower arrangement; dyeing and weaving; *maki-e* lacquerware decoration; wall-panel and screen paintings; residential and castle architecture, etc. Indeed, throughout the entire span of Japanese history, this period saw more remarkable changes and accomplishments than any other. This is Japan's third phase, a phase of "upheaval"; it too lasted for 450 years (1150-1600 CE).

With the transition into the Edo Era, Japanese civilization entered a period of stability and prosperity. Japan under the Tokugawa regime was the strongest centralized police and military state in the nation's history, with all authority concentrated at the center. Transportation routes were improved and expanded, weights and measures were unified nationwide, Tokugawa currency was introduced nationwide, a commodity market was unified nationwide, and the economy accrued unprecedented vibrancy. Prosperous urban centers developed—most notably Edo (later Tokyo), Osaka and Kyoto, with Edo encompassing a population of over one million people, qualifying it as the largest city in the world at the time. Education spread not only to the warrior class but to the general populace as well, and the literacy rate is said to have been the highest in the world. Developments were also achieved in diverse areas of learning—agriculture, herbal medicine, mathematics, Confucian philosophy, national philology and phi-

The Formation of Feudalism

losophy, national history, geography, etc.—and a wide array of publications, including encyclopedias, were produced. This was a period when Japan ranked as a world empire, just as had the preceding New Kingdom of Egypt, Han-period China, the Roman Empire, and India during the Gupta Period. This period as a world empire continued throughout the Edo Era (1600-1868) and is said to remain under way today.

The foregoing is a sketch of the progression of Japanese civilization through its different phases. The fact that it consists of four phases, plus the fact that each phase continued over a period of four to five centuries, are traits shared in common by all eight major civilizations. The features of its historical trends—for example in terms of politics, economics, social structure, culture, education and scientific learning—are also, to one degree or another, equally recognizable particularly within type A major civilizations.

Insofar as feudalism is concerned, the law-based *ritsuryō* state that appeared in Japan's second phase corresponds to unified states such as Europe's Carolingian Empire, China's Western Zhou state and Egypt's Old Kingdom. In each instance these states grew out of tribal confederations headed by a singular monarch, and without exception they all collapsed within a century or two, their land territories split asunder, and fragmentation continued throughout the subsequent third phase, a period of disturbance. It is this fragmented state that is referred to as feudalism.

Based on the foregoing, we can arrive at the following interpretation of the formation of feudal systems. At their genesis, type A major civilizations formed small-scale states of tribal federations, and around this core the states gradually expanded into centralized states covering wide areas. However, given the immature social conditions of an inherent lack of developed road and transport networks and an inadequately working barter economy, sustaining the centralized system of an expansive state on a continuing basis is impossible. Before long the unified hold loosens and the original regionalism in the form of tribes each ruling their own lands comes to the fore—a situation equating to feudalism. In other words, feudalism is the reemergence of the inherent state of tribes each governing their own territories. Still, this refers only to the underlying base; what must also be considered are the facts that a) civilizations undergo continuous growth and b) societies retain the memory of having previously been a brilliant unified state, and thriving on that ideal they aspire to revert to such unification. As far as this point is concerned, although I speak of a "reemergence," I am not referring to a simple return to the first phase or to the state of an undeveloped society of the kind that existed prior to the appearance of civilization; rather, what I mean is tribal regionalism of a higher level materialistically, intellectually and perceptively.

The Formation of Feudalism

At this point the question arises as to why, in spite of their immature social conditions, there appeared expansive unified states prior to the formation of feudal systems. One answer offered is what Hintze referred to as a propensity stemming from models of world-historical imperialism; but given the existence of examples where such a model is lacking, as in the cases of China and Egypt, another answer must be sought. In my view, it is appropriate to suggest that in the process of undergoing territorial expansion the tribal confederations came into contact and conflict with other peoples, and this aroused in them an awareness of the existence of a form of nation that transcends tribal parameters, leading them to create a large state extending to the limits of their borders.

In addition to Japan, Europe, China and Egypt, Peru too is a type A major civilization. The reason I did not discuss it earlier is because Peruvian civilization left behind no written materials and its chronology is dependent solely on archeological materials, as a result of which many details remain unclear. From that chronology, however, we know that starting around 200 CE Peruvian civilization passed through four phases each lasting roughly four centuries. First a major religious force was formed based at Tiwanaku (Tiahuanaco) in modern-day Bolivia; next came the unified state known as the Wari (Huari) Empire, which covered an even broader area; this was followed by a feudal situation in which small states arose in profusion; and finally history saw the building of the Inca Empire, a centralized military and police state that was the strongest in history and encompassed the largest territory in history. Records often speak of gradual technological progress and of the growth of urban centers and the robustness of commercial and industrial activities during the feudal period. As such, the argument is thus supported that the feudalism of Peru falls in line with the feudal systems common to other type A major civilizations.

Comparisons with Type B Societies

If feudalism is a phenomenon of type A major civilizations, one would expect to see a similar phenomenon in type B major civilizations as well.

The Sumerian, Greco-Roman and Indian civilizations belong to this type B. The four phases they each passed through consisted of the parallel existence of tribal states, the parallel existence of city-states, an interim period of disturbance, and development into a world empire. Where these differ from type A major civilizations is in the absence of political unity crowned by a singular monarch during the first and second phases. No suggestion has ever been made to date that feudalism existed within any of these type B civilizations.

However, as suggested by the fact that the various Sumerian cities shared common gods as well as their holy capital of Nippur, and also by the fact that the various Greek cities shared the perception of one national territory known as "Hellas," social and cultural unity was recognized early on. The fact that they are seen to have cherished the ideal of ultimately achieving political unity is identical to the case of type A major civilizations; also identical is the fact that they are viewed not as an extension of undeveloped small tribes but rather as regional separatism on top of a thick layer of material and spiritual culture that gradually built up throughout the entire social realm over the course of its history. In short, the basic structures of the time period in question can be said to be no different from that of type A major civilizations. Furthermore, in matters of detail also similarities undeniably exist—as demonstrated by the fact that early on Max Weber referred to the ancient Greek *polis* system as a feudal system for the reasons that citizens' rights coincided with the right to bear arms, perfect citizens were normally lords of estates, and patronage relationships based on religious passion (piety) formed the basis of the power of the dominant class. This pseudo-feudalism seen in type B societies can be said to all the more justify interpreting feudalism from the perspective of the major civilizations.

Type A major civilizations differ from type B in two ways: in being a tribal federation headed by a single monarch, and in developing into a unified state featuring objective institutional systems. With these traits of type A kept in mind, this unified state and despotic ruler naturally figure into the background of the ideal type of feudalism we set down separately. This is because in type A major civilizations the inviolable authority vested in the god-king pervaded thoroughly throughout their state system, locally fragmented power, and status-based domination.

However, I believe we should avoid infusing the ideal type of feudalism into type A major civilizations or deducing feudalism's ideal type from type A major civilizations and manipulating it in any minor ways. The ideal type of feudalism should maintain neutrality open to all cases as a form that is independent from specific examples.

Based on our perception that specific examples of genuine feudal systems coincide precisely with type A major civilizations, from the foregoing we can thus conclude that the answer to our present question—what was the driving force behind the formation of feudal systems?—is that it was the power of the civilization itself, and not, as Hintze suggested, any external power.

CHAPTER THREE

Transition from Feudalism to Capitalism

Causes of Feudalism's Decline

Maurice Dobb (1900-1976) (*Studies in the Development of Capitalism*, 1946) attributes the decline of European feudalism less to the external factor of commercial influences and more to the internal factors of exploitation and suppression. He says that as the aristocracy grew in numbers and the extravagant lifestyle of the ruling class put them in need of increasingly greater revenues, they applied increasing pressures on producers (farmer peasants), eventually causing them to flee and disperse in large numbers, thereby eroding the sustainability of the feudal economy.

Paul Sweezy (1910-2004) (in *The Transition from Feudalism to Capitalism*, 1976) disagrees with Dobb's view, questioning whether the aristocracy expanded to the extent that increased revenue for the ruling class became necessary. Sweezy acknowledges that a luxurious lifestyle did indeed spread, but he says that it ultimately traces its origins to the development of commerce and cities—and these, he contends, cannot by any sense be construed as configurations of feudalism. Feudalism, Sweezy claims, lacks internal capacity to self-engender; it goes into motion only as a result of external forces. Sweezy cites and supports the view of Henri Pirenne (1862-1935), who said that commerce in Europe (under the Frankish Empire) went into decline when Mediterranean trade was cut off by Islamic invaders in the 7th and 8th centuries, as a result of which a feudal, manorial economy based on peasant-farmer labor became dominant. Then when Mediterranean trade resumed at its eastern and western ends in the 11th century, European commercial production got under way, giving rise to the rebirth of cities and the development of markets.

For the most part participants in the debate concerning the transition from feudalism to capitalism, which commenced with the conflicting arguments expounded by Dobb and Sweezy, took sides with Dobb's contention that feudalism's downfall stemmed from internal disputes. Dobb's theory, however, to a considerable extent is premised on the development of commerce and cities; and Dobb is thus no different from Sweezy in viewing the development of a commodity economy as a factor behind the decline of feudalism. Where the real issue lies, however, both in the case of Dobb and Sweezy, is that they see the development of commerce and cities as external to feudalism.

Isn't it conceivable that commerce and cities arose within a feudal system? In the case of Japanese feudalism, which closely resembles the feudalism of Europe, commerce and cities developed without any external forces. I believe that cities, commercial production and productivity growth all welled up within feudal societies. In Pirenne's view, feudalism in Europe began slipping into decline after the Arab closure of the Mediterranean ended, enabling commercial trade to revive and cities to regain their earlier vibrancy. My view is that the influence deriving from the Mediterranean region occurred on the back of internal development.

Rodney Hilton (1916-2002) supports Dobb's view. "Pressure by the ruling class...was the root cause of the technical progress and improved feudal organisation which made for the enlargement of the disposable surplus. This was the basis for the growth of simple commodity production, seigneurial incomes in cash, international luxury trade and urbanisation," he wrote. Then again: "Peasant resistance was of crucial importance in the development of the rural communes, the extension of free tenure and status, the freeing of peasant and artisan economies for the development of commodity production and eventually the emergence of the capitalist entrepreneur." Although what he says is on the mark, the opposite can also be said: that commerce and cities set the stage for pressures by the ruling class, and money, freedom and individualism gave rise to peasant resistance. One is thus not the cause and the other its result; rather, one should think in terms of a moving body in which both exist as the cause and result of the other. I believe it is correct to view these phenomena within an irreversible flow of history moving in a particular direction.

In this chapter I will address the issue of identifying the forces that led to the breakdown of medieval feudal society in Europe and precipitated the creation of a modern capitalist civil society. The conclusion drawn from the foregoing suggests the answer is a particular strength found in European society—what Werner Sombart (1863-1941) defined as the "Faustian spirit" innate in Europeans and Max Weber called Europe's unique "rational spirit."

Faustian Spirit

In his Der Moderne Kapitalismus (1902) Werner Sombart writes that modern capitalism has its roots deep in the European spirit. At the base of that spirit exists a drive, difficult to define, to plunge forward, forcefully impose one's will, and conquer and dominate the world, crushing and vanquishing all hindrances along the way in a quest that recognizes no limits. This unlimited and this-worldly quest—what might be called the "Faustian spirit"—drove Europeans to undertake new creative pursuits within all realms of culture during the pre-modern era: in the realm of nation-building, feats of conquest and domination; in religion, acts of salvation and liberation; in science, achievements in elucidation and illumination; in technology, successes in invention and discovery; in earthly exploration, accomplishments of discovery. Within the realm of economics, the Faustian spirit was manifested as entrepreneurial greed aimed at securing controlling stakes, greed that shattered the framework of a self-sufficient medieval handicraft-based economy and gave birth to a profit-oriented economy seeking unlimited monetary benefit. Nothing is more appropriate for pursuit of the unlimited than the pursuit of value symbols in the form of abstract money—money liberated from organic, natural limitations.

Besides this Faustian entrepreneurial spirit, Sombart also refers to a civic spirit that brings to modern economic life a firmly established order, calculated validity, and levelheaded purposefulness. He labels the consolidation of these two spirits as the "capitalist spirit," and he says that this spirit is the creative force behind capitalism.

Mention of Faust brings to mind Goethe's play by that name, but the Faust who actually existed in the pages of history was a German who lived in the 16th century.

Johann Faust is said to have been an itinerant astrologer and alchemist who astonished his compatriots with his knowledge of natural science, medicine and psychology. In the 16th and 17th centuries numerous stories and plays were written throughout Europe based on his life. The Faust in these tales is said to have flown between earth and heaven on the wings of an eagle. Driven by the desires to know everything there is to know about the world, to acquire powers to make everything possible, to secure wealth and power, and to experience every pleasure there is to enjoy, he makes a pact with Satan that enables him to satisfy his desires; but as punishment for his haughtiness in trying to be God's equal, in the end he gets sent to hades. In Goethe's tragedy, however, instead of being dispatched to hell Faust ends with his soul being saved, the writer thus implicitly expressing approval of the Faustian spirit.

Sombart says the drive that propelled Faust is an instinctive impetus extant subconsciously at the root base of Western Europeans. This is difficult for us Japanese to understand immediately, and ours is at best only an indirect understanding based on the fact that the Faust theme remained popular into the 20th century and on our direct experience of the remarkable frailness of nature in Europe. Another individual who, like Sombart, sought to explain European culture using the example of Faust was Oswald Spengler (1880-1936). As a narrative, his *Der Untergang des Abendlandes* (The Decline of the

West, 1918-1922) is far more detailed, vivid, appealing and convincing.

In connection with mathematics, for example, Spengler says that Western mathematics is mathematics of functions in which numbers exist purely as relationships. Greek mathematics recognizes natural numbers (positive integers) only, and it is the concept of functions that overturns the statuesquely ordered array of specific, static numbers and develops and resolves them into a limitless continuum. This, Spengler contends, is the world sentiment of Westerners who perceive visible things as limited to the limitless, i.e. as a secondary reality. With respect to art, Spengler points out that Greek painting has foregrounds only; it does not have the clouds or horizons featured in Western painting. He says the horizon fusing heaven and earth in an unrealistic mist is the total sum of distances, it contains infinitesimal principles of painting, and it is from here that the "fugue" of painting flows forth. In Greek mythology, Mount Olympus, abode of the gods, is situated in close proximity on Greek territory; but in Germanic mythology, Walhalla, residence of the gods, floats in some dark and distant nowhere transcending all perceptual realities, lost in a limitless world where unsociable deities and heroes appear as supreme symbols of solitude.

Innately therefore, Spengler says that Westerners are born with a Faustian spirit, a sentiment that admits no constraints, is manifested by a strong will, and wanders over long distances. It is typically contrasted with the inborn apollonian sentiment of the Greeks, who cling to proximate bodies.

To fly is to liberate ourselves from our earthbound existence, to vanish beyond the far reaches of the universe; to fly is supremely Faustian, and the realization of our dreams. Christian painting indicates variations on this theme. Its depictions of ascent to heaven and descent into hell, of flights taken above the clouds, of the supreme bliss of angels and saints, and of release from all earthly gravity are all symbols of the Faustian spirit, and they are completely unknown in Byzantine art.

In the legal realm, in contrast to Greco-Roman law, which is no more than an amalgamation of individual judicial precedents based on real experiences, Western law, ever since the ancient *Sachsenspiegel*, has been law of functions that apply perpetually and cover all possibilities. Furthermore, in reference to the world of economics, Spengler says that in contrast to the Greco-Roman monetary concept which stopped at physical coinage, the monetary concept of the West was a concept of abstract functions that arise and move; supported by sources of energy, the spirit of invention, and the concept of trust, the Western monetary concept occupies a dynamic field covering the entire earth.

Although Spengler is well known for having made Faust the symbol of the innate sentiment of the Westerner, more than a decade earlier Sombart did likewise—even if only on a modest scale. That he did so is indicative of Sombart's superlative powers of insight.

My impression of Sombart is that he recognized a Faustian spirit of unbounded orientation only in reference to an entrepreneurial spirit; he treated it separately from a civic spirit that engenders an established order, calculated validity, and levelheaded purposefulness. I suggest, however, that it might be preferable to combine the two into one. I say this because the execution of reason from start to finish lies at the root of order, calculation and purposefulness, and it can be said to be a manifestation of unlimited pursuit, the sentiment of Faustian conquest and domination. Sombart, by incorporating what he called a civic spirit into Faustian spirit in that manner, achieves consistency with respect to what makes Faust Faust. Also, criticism of Sombart (by Max Weber), to the effect that there is no need to talk about a Faustian spirit because the unlimited pursuit of profit has existed everywhere since antiquity, loses its potency.

Rationalist Spirit

In the opening of his preface to *Gesammelte Aufsätze zur Religionssoziologie* (Collected Essays in the Sociology of Religion, 1920-1921) Max Weber wrote the following: "What chain of circumstances led to the appearance in the West, and only in the West, of cultural phenomena which—or so at least we like to think—came to have *universal* significance and validity?" To illustrate, he then offers up the examples of scientific learning, the arts, politics and economics.

In reference to scientific learning, he cites the formation of a mathematical basis, rational experimentation, systematic theology, rational concepts concerning state theory, and a strict legal form of thinking. In conjunction with the arts, he offers the example of rational harmonic music. In connection with state administration, he talks of political mechanisms in which bureaucrat specialists govern in accordance with rational rules. Concerning economics, Weber speaks of modern Europe's objective and rational forms of management, labor and markets; separation of household management and business management; and rational speculation and rational bookkeeping, in contrast to the *oikos* (household) type management and adventurous, get-rich-quick type speculation of other cultures.

As the item common to all such examples, Weber points to "rationalism," and he says that at the basis of this rationalization trend characteristic of Europe lies the rational lifestyle rooted in innate human nature. Within the realm of Western Christianity the Church formed as a unified, rational organization possessing both a monarchic leader and centralized control of faith; and parallel to this, otherworldly abstinence by members of religious orders gradually assumed a systematic structure as a methodology pursuant to a positive lifestyle. This then led, in the context of Protestantism, to the introduction of rational abstinence in secular life. In contrast to this pragmatic rationalism characteristic of Western faith and its methodical organization of an external lifestyle, within all popular religions in Asia the earthly world is a great magical garden, a place where spirit worship, magic, mystical meditation, and a sacramental quest for salvation have been carried out.

The foregoing observations by Weber concerning rationalism — rationalism that is unique to European culture and, as such, gives that culture its universality — accord with the thinking of Georg Hegel (1770-1831), who purported that a rational mentality, as it slowly proceeded westward, underwent its foremost self-manifestation in the Germanic European realm. In *Die Protestantische Ethik und der Geist des Kapitalismus* (The Protestant Ethic and the Spirit of Capitalism, 1904-1905) Max Weber wrote that for Puritans, primarily Calvinists, of the 16th and 17th centuries profit-making became an ethical obligation; they pursued systematic and rational profit and a corresponding attitude toward life, and this became the driving force that promoted modern capitalism. As demonstrated by the wealth of criticism voiced by many over the course of history, this view centered on Protestantism seems inadequate as an explanation for the driving force behind modern capitalism; however, if its faith and lifestyle are viewed within the context of the rationalization movement present in European culture as a whole, the argument takes on greater breadth and depth, thereby serving to weaken the force of such criticism.

When Weber's rational spirit is compared to the Faustian spirit espoused by Sombart and Spengler, although both are the underlying nature of culture, one can say that the latter is larger and more profound and subsumes the former. As I just noted, reason is a component factor of the Faustian spirit. Reason collides with and penetrates all sorts of specific, organic things, pulverizes them, moves them about freely, and gives order to abstract concepts. Modern Europe's discovery of new worlds, its numerous inventions and discoveries made in the natural sciences, and its invasion and plunder of other continents are, as Sombart said, the biggest factors that spurred the development of modern capitalism; and it seems more appropriate to attribute these to a Faustian impulse rather than to reason.

Actually, the rational spirit spoken of by Weber corresponds to what, as noted earlier, Sombart referred to as a civic spirit that brings to modern economic life a firmly established order, calculated validity, and level-headed purposefulness. Weber is critical of Sombart's *Der Moderne Kapitalismus*. He says that what is unique to modern Europe, i.e. the presence of rational labor organizations, weakens in this work remarkably, and developmental factors (the unlimited pursuit of profit) that have worked continuously all over the world since ancient times are pushed to the forefront. This is by no means the case, however; Sombart assigned to rational spirit the role of sustaining half the whole of modern capitalism.

Is There Only One "Modern Capitalism"?

Sombart, Spengler and Weber all attribute to a Faustian or rational spirit the power that broke down medieval feudal society and gave birth to modern capitalism. For them, and for nearly all scholars, capitalism is something that is unique to the West: they contend that the Faustian spirit or rational inclination unique to the West gave rise to an economic system that likewise is unique to the West. Marx and Marxists also, without mentioning Faust or rationalization, similarly reject any notion of relativization, and they view capitalism as something absolute that appeared only in the West. While granting that other systems of economic development — Asiatic, slave-based, feudal — are found in other regions, they say capitalism is something that is limited to the West only.

What would happen, though, if we were to assume that modern capitalism arose not only in the West but also independently in other regions as well? To propose this hypothesis contrary to the conventional wisdom, it would be necessary either to recognize a Faustian spirit or rational inclination in other peoples or to assume that Western capitalism was driven by a force different from these.

This hypothesis depends on the assumption made about modern capitalism. If that assumption is flexible, the hypothesis becomes possible; but if the assumption approaches limitation to one specific example, such a hypothesis gradually becomes impossible. Until now, no attempt has ever been made to view modern capitalism from such a broad perspective. Modern capitalism has always been equated with Europe, and even when similar examples have been reported, they have been treated as germinant forms or fragments. They have in all instances been compared against the characteristics of capitalism specific to the West, and ultimately been rejected.

The capitalism I am referring to is not capitalism in the sense simply of entrepreneurial greed or profit-seeking as spoken of by Lujo Brentano (1844-1931) or Henri Pirenne. Capitalism of that ilk is found everywhere, in times both old and new. The capitalism I have in mind is the economy of ancient Rome, the economy of Han-period China, the economy of Tokugawa Japan. That these are unrelated or unworthy of comparison to modern capitalism or industrial capitalism is a notion I absolutely refuse to believe. Considering them to be mere germinant forms or fragments also seems virtually inconceivable unless one endeavors to make exhaustive inquiries.

The attempt I made in chapter 1 to create an ideal type of feudalism was based on combined assessments of feudalism's numerous definitions and of the various societies conventionally said to be feudal. In the case of industrial capitalism, however, because there are said to be no examples similar to the Western form, one is compelled to determine the true sense of industrial capitalism based solely on a conceptual weight comparison keeping in mind the various extant definitions rooted in Western capitalism. The only result that emerges from this is knowing whether or not there existed economic systems closely related to modern Western capitalism.

Essential Nature of Modern Capitalism

How has modern capitalism been defined until now? Here I will summarize the widely known views proposed by Marx, Bücher, Sombart and Weber.

Marx differentiates economic systems according to their respective modes of production, with a focus on the manner of ownership of the production means by direct producers. In the Asiatic mode of production, direct producers own their production means—land, tools, etc.—outright. In Greco-Roman and feudal production modes, ownership is only partial. In the modern civil mode of production, i.e., in capitalism, there is no ownership. In modern capitalism, the direct producers are proletarians possessing no land, tools or other property; they sell their only possession — their labor capacity — on the market and make products they cannot themselves own. Capitalists increase their capital through the surplus value thus engendered. In this way, in the Marxist context the mark of modern capitalism is wage-based commodity-producing labor by an unpropertied class working on behalf of the capitalist class at the opposite end of the social spectrum.

In the view of Karl Bücher (1847-1930), modern economy belongs to the national economy phase characterized by production and broad circulation of goods; it contrasts with its two preceding phases — an independent household economy consisting wholly of production for one's own needs, and a medieval town economy limited to custom production within a narrow economic sphere. As defining characteristics of national economy, Bücher also cites wage-based labor under free contract, separation of business and household sectors, economic sovereignty of movable capital in lieu of land, factory-based industry in place of work in the home or handicraft manufacture, permanent places of commerce in place of itinerant peddling or market commerce, and erosion of sentiment-based social interactions.

In Sombart's view, modern capitalism is a distribution-based economic system in which owners of the production means (the economic subject) and unpropertied laborers (the economic object) join forces and cooperate within the market—an economic system dominated by commercialism and economic rationalism. In the self-sufficient economy and handicraft manufacture-based economy that preceded it, there is neither the social differentiation nor conflicting linkage of this human production factor, no commercialism aimed at monetary expansion, and no economic rationalism incorporating management planning, purposeful intent and a calculating aspect.

Weber stresses the rational aspect of modern capitalism. In his view, the markers of modern capitalism include a rational pursuit of profit, management and speculation based on accurate planning and evaluation, a rational organization of free labor, separation of household and business management, and rational bookkeeping. Weber contends that in the final analysis modern capitalism differs fundamentally from adventure capitalism, mercantile capitalism, or capitalism that targets acquisition of profit through political gains or warfare. Ultimately, Weber says, modern capitalism equates to civil, managerial capitalism having a rational organization of free labor.

An overview of the foregoing definitions indicates that, alongside commercialistic production of commodities two elements are emphasized as distinguishing characteristics of modern capitalism: wage-based labor by an unpropertied labor force, and rational and measurable management and organization. Whereas the former is stressed by Marx and the latter by Weber, Sombart integrates the two — following precedent in one instance and setting a precedent in the other. Insofar as which of these two elements is today considered the more essential to modern capitalism, the prevailing trend of commentary to date seems, as far as I am aware, to lean in favor of Marx's view — and I wish to concur with that assessment. I do so because while the structure of production is a decisive factor in an economic system and wage-based labor is a constituent element requisite to a modern capitalistic production structure, rationality is an attribute of labor that increases production efficiency.

Keeping the foregoing discussion of the essential nature of modern capitalism in mind, I will now take under review the capitalist systems of ancient Rome, Han-dynasty China and Japan in the late Edo Period — systems that are all on occasion said to be modern in nature.

The Debate over Ancient Capitalism

There is a long history to the debate as to whether or not the ancient Greek and Roman societies were capitalist in a modern sense. The debate began with a refutation of Karl Bücher's contention by Eduard Meyer (1855-1930). I touched upon Bücher's view above, but to describe it in more detail, in his *Die Entstehung der Volkswirtschaft* (The Rise of National Economy, 1893)

Bücher differentiates three general stages of economic development: an independent domestic economy, a town economy, and national economy.

By an independent domestic economy Bücher refers to a closed economy where there exists no exchange, an economy in which goods are consumed entirely internally. In Greek and Roman societies, for example, economic matters were confined to the household and did not extend beyond it. Social relationships too were limited to inter-family relationships and there were no interpersonal relations. There were no class distinctions, no peasant farmers and no handicraft workers—only a gap between the wealthy and the poor.

In a town economy, goods are produced for customers and directly traded, moving from the economy where they are produced directly to the economy where they are consumed. Medieval Europe is taken as a classic example. Here, labor was divided among farmers, craftsmen and traders, and there also arose class distinctions. Self-sufficiency remained strong, however; there were no permanent enterprises; and capital was limited to mercantile capital.

National economy is an economy marked by wholesale production and circulation of goods, an economy in which goods are produced commercially and pass through a number of economic spheres before they are consumed. National economy is a product of the centralization of political power that took place in Europe after the late medieval period. In addition to commercial capital, this phase gave rise to lending capital; this then developed into capital loaned in advance to village industry; and this led to manufacturing and mass production in factories adopting division of labor, along with which there arose a class of wage-earning workers.

Meyer refuted this view of Bücher's in *Die Wirtschaftliche Entwicklung des Altertums* [The Economic Development of Antiquity] (in *Jahrbücher für Nationalokonomie und Statistik* [Journal of Economics and Statistics], Bd. IX, 1895). He argued that it was quite impossible to place the economies of Greece and Rome within the category of a domestic economy. In the case of Greece after the 8th century BCE, he cited its monetary economy, the formation and spread of commerce and industry, and the existence of status-based classes. In the case of the Hellenistic and Roman periods, he pointed to their operation of large-scale slave-labored farms, their flourishing international trade, formation of large cities, and expansion of a proletarian class. Particularly in the case of the post-Hellenistic era, this, Meyer contends, should be seen as corresponding to the national economy phase.

This debate was subsequently carried on between economic historians and scholars of ancient history, with both sides presenting a variety of arguments. And while even today the debate cannot be said to have come to any final conclusions, in the process the view advocated by Max Weber is considered to be the work that clarified the theoretical basis of the debate and handed down an objective assessment of both camps.

In Weber's view, the self-sufficient household economy spoken of by Bücher and his predecessor Karl Rodbertus (1805-1875) inarguably played an important role in ancient societies in general, but insofar as Greek and Roman societies are concerned, it was a feature of the early and late periods only. Regarding the vast slave property of their heydays, Weber says the view of Meyer is correct. In ancient times furthermore, the existence of free peasants, free craftsmen, and free unskilled wage laborers is in general broadly recognized, and Weber contends that these cannot be dealt with entirely relying on Bücher's concept of a domestic economy. At the same time, however, Weber argues that Meyer's view is incorrect in attempting to manipulate Athens' golden period using such altogether modern concepts as "factories" and "factory workers." Weber says there is no evidence of the existence of what would be worthy of the name "factory operation" in terms of scale, duration in existence, division of labor, fixed assets, etc.; the *ergasterion* (workplace), he suggests, was no more than an amalgamation of slave labor. Commercial formats (maritime credit, commenda), bank payment operations and bank transfers as legal formats did not pass beyond the early medieval phase, and there was no separation of household and workplace, no separation between personal property and business property, and no permanent corporate format akin to a joint-stock company. Also, hoarded items of precious metal were used as capital only very rarely. For these reasons, Weber says it is precarious to assume that the economy of Greece was modern.

In presenting the foregoing argument, Weber says that ultimately the problem lies in how to define capitalism. He states that in the case of purely economic content in the form of usage of a tradable property by a private individual for the purpose of distributional economic type profit, capitalism can be recognized throughout antiquity; but when seen in the sense of incorporating social content in the form of usage of a labor force of free individuals under work contract, one must conclude that there was no capitalism as such. Today, capitalism is generally interpreted with a leaning toward perpetual large-scale business operation by private individuals making use of the labor of free persons — an operational format that did not exist in ancient times.

Weber's view can be summarized as follows.

1) The household economy is generally an appropriate interpretation of the economy of the Mediterranean world in antiquity. (Bücher's view is correct.)
2) If capitalism is taken to be business management with a distributional economic base, then capitalism can be recognized in the Mediterranean world throughout antiquity. (This erodes the viability of

Bücher's view.)
3) Large-scale business operation using slave labor as seen in Roman times shares some points in common with modern capitalism. (Meyer's view is correct.)
4) The general economic systems that existed in Greece and Rome during specific periods cannot be identified as modern capitalism. (Meyer's view is wrong.)

The last point is one that Weber stressed in particular.

Problems with Weber's View

One point in Weber's view that seems dubious is his contention that Meyer treated ancient economies in the category of modern economies. A careful examination of Meyer's work in question, *Die Wirtschaftliche Entwicklung des Altertums*, reveals that what Meyer aimed to say is not that he views Greece and Rome on equal terms with the modern West, but rather that, from the perspective of a cyclical view of history, certain periods in Greek and Roman history correspond to certain periods in Western history. Taking an overview of Greek and Roman history, Meyer offers a number of remarks to this effect concerning historical flows. For example, he states that Greece of the 6th and 7th centuries BCE corresponds to modern Western Europe during the 14th and 15th centuries, and Greece of the 5th century

BCE is akin to the 16th century in Western Europe. He also says that during the Hellenistic period there existed highly developed global communications and "national economy" in the sense intended by Bücher. Meyer further contends that a number of emerging trends—incessant warfare, penetration of slave-based economy into agriculture, deterioration of farming villages, influxes of farming village populations into large cities, the development of colossal capital and ownership of large estates, increased numbers in the unpropertied proletariat—all have profound meaning in contemporary times as well.

These are indications not of identical sameness between phenomena or formats of one kind or another, but indications of correspondences in historical phases. Meyer is not pointing to the presence of modern capitalism but to modern capitalistic phases. In discussions of historical phases, rather than individual phenomena or formats themselves, what is important is the overall picture. With this viewpoint, it becomes possible to think of capitalism not in terms of a sharp distinction between what Weber called "pariah capitalism" and modern capitalism. Rather, we can assume that there are societies in which many continuous stages exist between the two, which reach a point close to Western modern capitalism.

To Weber, this difference may not have great meaning. He entertains the firm belief that modern capitalism is altogether unique to Western Europe. If Meyer's true meaning is as I have just described, then it does conflict with Weber's argument—and this is the reason why he opposed Meyer so strongly. As a side note, when most Marxists discuss this debate over ancient capitalism, they tend to express support for Weber's view and declare Meyer the loser. But while they do so for their own reasons, different from Weber's, to explain capitalism's developmental phases, in their case too one can suggest that their conclusion is entwined with their underlying contention that modern capitalism is something unique to Western Europe.

Capitalism in Ancient Rome

Many of the materials and arguments presented to date in the debate over ancient capitalism—by Max Weber, Johannes Hasebroek (1893-1957), Erich Ziebarth (1868-1944), Hendrik Bolkestein (1877-1942), Aleksander Tjumenev (1890-1959) and Jakov Lencman (1908-1967), among others—have primarily concerned the classical period of ancient Greece, notably in the 5th century BCE. However, because throughout all of Greek and Roman history a capitalist economic aspect is actually recognized strongly in the time of the Roman Empire, I believe it may be possible to bring a swift resolution to the debate by shifting focus to the economy of ancient Rome.

In the days of the Roman Empire, Rome and Italy became the center of the world—and a huge marketplace. As a major center of consumption, Rome imported goods from many locations: from Egypt, grain, linen and jewels; from Syria, dyestuffs, glass and silk; from Asia Minor, wool, timber and iron; from Greece, olive oil and marble; from Spain, mineral products, woven fabrics and wool; from Gaul, grain and livestock products; and from the Danube region, iron, animal hides, horses and slaves. Meanwhile Italy also exported an array of industrial goods, including wine, olive oil, pottery, metal utensils and glassware.

Private manufacture of iron wares, bronze vessels, gold and silver crafted products, pottery, glassware and woven textiles, along with mining operations, was conducted broadly in Italy's regions and cities, and it is well established that there existed not only division of labor and specialization, but also production of goods unique to each region and city. In all of these industries, there are numerous examples of large-scale business operation, with anywhere from several dozen to several hundred slaves working under a system of labor division. Particularly in the mining industry, it was not unusual for even thousands of slaves to be employed simultaneously.

In the farming villages, in place of the society of Roman Republic days centered on independent farms of small to medium scale, during Rome's Imperial period land became concentrated in the hands of the aristocracy and *nouveau riche* merchants and manufacturers. Operation of large farms employing vast numbers of slaves became the norm, and production centered on such staple commodities as grapes, olives and livestock. In the process, the formerly independent farmers either went to ruin and became subordinate farmers, or became unpropertied proletarians and migrated into the cities.

In this way, the economy of the Roman Empire, by virtue of its elements of market-oriented production, mass production, a broad area of distribution, and free competition, closely resembles a modern economy. As such, it would seem altogether feasible to label such an economy "capitalism"; but in reality this is not the case. While free wage-earning laborers did exist, the fact that operations for the most part depended on slave labor is what is said to separate the Roman example markedly from a modern economy. In a nutshell, the two are dissimilar by dint of the simple assessment that a slave system does not equate to capitalism.

The mark of a modern economy is free wage labor. Slaves are neither free nor wage-earning laborers, so it is only natural to make a distinction. But in their respective essential qualities, are the two truly different?

Purchased slaves possess no means of production at all. Free laborers also possess no means of production. In both instances, they possess no property, and it is their labor capacity that is traded as a commodity in the market. The capitalist invests his capital into buying a production means along with such labor, uses them to produce commodities of some kind, and sells those commodities in the market as a way of realizing surplus value, thereby increasing his capital. Purchased slaves and free laborers are both providers of labor who occupy the same position and perform the same role within this circuit of capital. I would suggest that the two are identical in the crucial aspect of them both being providers of the commodity of labor. And compared to this "labor commodity," is not "freedom" lacking as a defining force?

Weber too was of this thinking, and this is why in the large slave operations of ancient Roman times he saw similarities with modern capitalism. Nevertheless, he did not identify the Roman situation as a modern economy because ultimately he also recognized in a slave-based economy a number of other differences. First, in the slave-based system the amount of investment is enormous and capital turnover is slow, thus making for significant risk. Second, prices fluctuate wildly depending on the presence or absence of war or on an outcome of victory or defeat, thereby undermining a basis of cost calculation—which makes modern, perpetual operation difficult. And third, owing to the lack of a sense of personal gain in slaves, technical progress and an accurate coupling of labor are impeded.

If, however, one does not give too much weight to this measurability and rationality stressed by Weber, but instead limits the matter to the structure of industrial capitalism, in which the labor force functions in the process of increasing capital, then fundamentally one would have to recognize in slave-based operations the same modern capitalist nature as in a free, labor-based system. I offer that the reason a slave-based system continued for so long in modern-day America alongside a free, labor-based system is because it shared this modern capitalist structure.

In a purchased slave-based system, one finds a reason why this system can be said to be more "modern" than a free, labor-based system. Although modern free laborers have no possessions, their ability to work is inherently their own, and they merely provide it by "leasing" it out. Purchased slaves' ability to work is inherently not their own, however, and for this reason their lack of possessions is more thorough. Given that the fundamental reason modern capitalism is "modern" consists largely of the laborer's having nothing whatsoever and his being subordinate to a capitalist, one must say that because the modern laborer is a free individual, the slave-based system is more modern capitalistic in nature than modern capitalism.

In ancient Rome, there were no mechanized factories, only a weak separation between the household and business, no formation of enterprises resembling joint-stock companies and thus no perpetuation of such, and rational labor organizations were lacking. This is beyond argument. However, if one looks at these elements only as qualitative fortification and quantitative expansion, then one should be able to consider the Roman economy much closer to modern capitalism than before.

The foregoing understanding of slave labor differs also from the interpretation espoused by Marx. According to Marx, the modern laborer sells his labor only during given time frames; if he were to sell it in its entirety at one time, he would change from a free individual to a slave, and from the owner of a commodity to a commodity itself. In this way, Marx differentiates between a modern laborer and a purchased slave based on the single point of "freedom." In terms of the process of producing surplus value, however, how much meaning is there in the difference between the laborer being the possessor of the commodity of labor and being the commodity of labor itself? Also, at the basis of the differences among economic systems Marx points to the producer's possession of objective conditions of production (tools, livestock, etc.), and he raises the issue of their gradual loss within the historical process of going from a primitive community to a contemporary society. In doing so he treats slaves, like cattle, as an objective condition of production itself conquered as a whole along with land and excludes them from the historical lineage of the loss. This way of understanding conflicts with my view, which sees slaves as direct producers and makes an issue of the slaves' ownership or non-ownership of objective conditions of production. In my view, slaves inevitably, insofar as they are total losers of objective conditions of production, are akin to modern laborers. At times, though, Marx refers to the modern wage-based labor system as a system of indirect slavery or wage-based slavery. I think one can probably see this as an indication that he does so, in spite of his foregoing contention, because he recognized a certain degree of shared traits in their respective internal structures.

"The Biographies of the Money-makers"

Scholars of Chinese history often note the presence of capitalist aspects within the economy of the Han Dynasty. A source they frequently cite is Sima Qian's (ca. 145-ca. 90 BCE) *Shi Ji* (Records of the Grand Historian): specifically chapter 129: "The Biographies of the Money-makers."

Here, Sima Qian lists commodities for which various regions are known:

"The region west of the mountains is rich in timber, bamboo, paper mulberry, hemp, oxtails for banner tassels, jade and other precious stones. That east of the mountains abounds in fish, salt, lacquer, silk, singers, and beautiful women. The area south of the Yangtze produces camphor wood, catalpa, ginger, cinnamon, gold, tin, lead ore, cinnabar, rhinoceros horns, tortoise shell, pearls of various shapes, and elephant tusks and hides, while that north of Longmen

and Jieshi is rich in horses, cattle, sheep, felt, furs, tendons, and horns."

— Translation by Burton Watson, page 434

Sima Qian also records the biographies of individuals who made fortunes as merchants or producers—people like Fan Li, Zigong, Bai Gui, Yin Dun, Guo Zong and Wuzhi Luo—and introduces various commercial cities, including Handan, Yan, Luoyang, Linzi and Suiyang. Particularly noteworthy is the historian's depiction of commodities that permit an individual to reap an income of "200,000 cash"—like a "lord of 1,000 households":

"Thus it is said that those who own pasture lands producing fifty horses a year, or 100 head of cattle, or 500 sheep, or 500 marshland swine; those who own reservoirs stocked with 1,000 piculs of fish or mountain lands containing 1,000 logs of timber; those who have 1,000 jujube trees in Anyi, or 1,000 chestnut trees in Yan or Qin, or 1,000 citrus trees in Shu, Han, or Jiangling, or 1,000 catalpas north of the Huai River or south of Changshan in the region of the Yellow and Qi rivers; those who own 1,000 mu of lacquer trees in Chen or Xia, 1,000 mu of mulberries or hemp in Qi or Lu, or 1,000 mu of bamboo along the Wei River; those who own farmlands in the suburbs of some famous capital or large city which produce one zhong of grain per mu, or those who own 1,000 mu of gardenias or madder

for dyes, or 1,000 beds of ginger or leeks—all these may live just as well as a marquis enfeoffed with 1,000 households. Commodities such as these are in fact the sources of considerable wealth. Their owners need not visit the market place or travel about to other cities but may simply sit at home and wait for the money to come in."

—*Ibid., page 448*

The cited passage implies the investment of capital into a business having promise and engagement in production on one's own terms. Accordingly, as a type of capital this is neither merchant's capital, in which case profit is reaped on trade alone, nor usurer's capital, with which profit is gained through lending at a high interest rate; rather, it is industrial capital, funds employed to earn profit through production.

Sima Qian discusses merchant's capital and usurer's capital elsewhere:

"Anyone who in the market towns or great cities manages in the course of a year to sell the following items: 1,000 brewings of liquor; 1,000 jars of pickles and sauces; 1,000 jars of syrups; 1,000 slaughtered cattle, sheep, and swine; 1,000 zhong of grain; 1,000 cartloads or 1,000 boat-lengths of firewood and stubble for fuel; 1,000 logs of timber; 10,000 bamboo poles; 100 horse carriages; 1,000 two-wheeled ox carts; 1,000 lacquered wooden vessels; brass utensils weighing 30,000 catties; 1,000 piculs of plain

wooden vessels, iron vessels, or gardenia and madder dyes; 200 horses; 500 cattle; 2,000 sheep or swine; 100 male or female slaves; 1,000 catties of tendons, horns, or cinnabar; 30,000 catties of silken fabric, raw silk, or other fine fabrics; 1,000 rolls of embroidered or patterned silk; 1,000 piculs of fabrics made of vegetable fiber or raw or tanned hides; 1,000 pecks of lacquer; 1,000 jars of leaven or salted bean relish; 1,000 catties of globefish or mullet; 1,000 piculs of dried fish; 30,000 catties of salted fish; 3,000 piculs of jujubes or chestnuts; 1,000 skins of fox or sable; 1,000 piculs of lamb or sheep skins; 1,000 felt mats; or 1,000 zhong of fruits or vegetables—such a man may live as well as the master of an estate of 1,000 chariots. The same applies for anyone who has 1,000 strings of cash (i.e., 1,000,000 cash) to lend out on interest. Such loans are made through a money-lender, but a greedy merchant who is too anxious for a quick return will only manage to revolve his working capital three times while a less avaricious merchant has revolved his five times."

—*Ibid., page 449*

With industrial capital, labor is a critical issue; but in relation to this matter, no detailed material exists. It is often said, however, that such labor was performed by the ruined peasants or transient populations that grew in numbers as the wealthy merchants and affluent farmers increasingly annexed new lands. In such situations, the workforce consisted of subordinate dependents or freely contracted wage larborers. *Yantielun* (Discourses on Salt and Iron, 1st CBE), a record loosely recording a debate that occurred during the Han Dynasty, describes how large, powerful, wealthy families amassed over 1,000 itinerants and put them to work excavating iron ore or boiling water to collect salt. *Han Shu* (Book of Han) records how the wife of Zhang Anshi (d. 62 BCE) used 700 house servants to operate a spinning and weaving business that brought her great financial wealth. At the very least, the former of these two cases must be said to embody the structure of industrial capital.

Kiyoyoshi Utsunomiya (1905-1998), in his *Kandai shakai-keizaishi kenkyū* (Studies on the Socio-economic History of the Han Dynasty, 1955), wrote, "Since remote antiquity Chinese culture has been developing, reaching a stage of completion, and developing further, and it was in the Qin and Han dynasties that it encountered periods of great completion." The reason the Han Dynasty was for a long time looked up to by posterity as a classical period inarguably owed to its nature, as Utsunomiya said, as a great completion and grand conclusion of that long history and culture.

Within the area of economics also, the Han Dynasty has the aspect of a point of conclusion after a lengthy process of development. Industrial activities began in the Spring and Autumn Period, when industries arose that produced bronze vessels, articles of jade, silk fabrics, etc., and a military industry (construction of citadels, etc. and production of armor and chariots of war) developed. In the Warring States Period, with the dissemination of iron farm tools and the introduction of land cultivation by plow, agricultural production rose dramatically, a commodity economy spread throughout the territory, and not only handicraft industries such as leather, pottery, carpentry and textiles but even large-scale industries producing iron and salt came to be privately operated. The economic sphere expanded to encompass nearly the entire territory of the seven states within one sphere of circulation, land and water transport systems developed, and commercial cities developed at strategic points along the transport routes.

With the unification of the whole country during the Qin and Han dynasties, the entire national territory was melded into one tightly knit economic sphere, transport routes spread in all directions, and commercial trade extended as far as India and Central Asia. The aforementioned *Yantielun* records that many large cities flourished along the transport routes, many merchants gathered at these centers, and goods of all kinds were being produced.

The economy recorded in the "The Biographies of the Money-makers" is the product of this economic development. Here, I wish to call attention to two facts. One is the fact that the economic prosperity was not a temporary and ephemeral bloom, but rather a firm outcome of self-sustaining development. The other is that this economy closely approached modern economy not only in its external aspects—i.e., a broad-based transport network, large cities, international trade, large-scale industries, large land ownership, and increasing numbers of the unpropertied resulting from the breakdown of the farmer peasant class—but also in the qualitative aspect of the existence of industrial capital over a broad area.

Manufacture Controversy

Japanese society during the Edo Period clearly showed aspects closely resembling those of the Roman and Han societies just described, as well as those of modern European society. It had highly developed cities nationwide, including the three main urban centers of Edo (Tokyo), Osaka and Kyoto; an expanding network of major roads, exemplified by the "Five Routes" (Tōkaidō, Nakasendō, Kōshu Kaidō, Ōshu Kaidō, Nikkō Kaidō); a well-developed communications system (courier post); cultivation of cash crops in areas near major cities; well-developed industries in mining, smelting, salt production, spinning, etc.; sophisticated commercial organizations, as seen in the formation of guilds of wholesalers; a unified system of weights and measures, and a unified currency; production of large volumes of commodities and a unified national market; highly developed financial institutions (money changers) performing banking functions including deposit accounts, lending, currency exchange and issuance of drafts; wholesale and speculative markets; the emergence of a strong class of townsmen and large numbers of affluent tradesmen; and stratification of farmer peasants, annexation of lands, and flows of ruined peasants into major cities.

As in the Han case, this economy was the fruit of a gradual process of development spanning several centuries. And while examples showing aspects such as these as the developmental stages are extremely rare within the 5,000 years of world history and thus its existence itself is surprising, Japan went beyond the Han and Roman examples and had the air suggesting it had reached the same stage of development as Western Europe in modern times. Many people may be familiar with Japan, but few in the world know that it possesses a history of this kind.

In the first half of the 20th century a well-known—well-known in Japan, that is—controversy erupted concerning this matter: the so-called "manufacture controversy."

The point at issue in the manufacture controversy was the suggestion that not only Europe but Japan too had spontaneously reached the manufacturing stage by the latter years of the Edo Period. Manufacture is a configuration of capitalist production immediately preceding the emergence of large-scale machine industry from the Industrial Revolution; it is defined as production, applying manufacturing skills, by a considerable number of laborers working in a factory under a system of co-operation based on division of labor. A classic example is said to be the woolen manufacturing industry of England that arose in the second half of the 16th century and continued for 200 years.

The manufacture controversy began as an exchange between Shisō Hattori (1901-1956) and Takao Tsuchiya (1896-1988). Subsequently other historians joined in, and the controversy persisted until the mid-20th century.

Hattori elaborated his views in a number of treatises published in the 1930s: most notably, *Meiji ishin no kakumei oyobi hankakumei* (Revolutionary and Anti-Revolutionary Aspects of the Meiji Restoration), *Ishinshi hōhōjō no shomondai* (Methodological Problems in Restoration History), *Hōhō to zairyō no mondai* (Problems of Methods and Materials) and *Genmitsu na imi de no manyufakuchua jidai* (The Age of Manufacture Proper). His contentions spelled out in those works are as follows.

Generally speaking, Hattori says, the conventional view concerning the economic stage of the late Edo Period is that small-scale farming, rural domestic industry and handicraft industry prevailed, and that at best it was in a process of accumulating commercial capital and usurious capital, i.e., it had not yet, by any measure, reached the stage of capitalism. According to this view, the chief cause of the production method reforms undertaken in the Meiji Period was outside force in the form of foreign commodities. However, capitalist domestic labor (putting-out system) was carried out widely; piecework as a side job performed by low-class samurai, which was a common custom in castle towns, can be said to be the de facto hired labor undertaken by capitalists; and in industries including metal refining, silk reeling, textiles, ceramics and brewing, manufacture was distributed to a considerable degree in rural areas. Particularly in the case of the silk-reeling and textile industries of places like Kaga, Kiryu and Ashikaga (in what are today, respectively, Ishikawa, Gunma and Tochigi prefectures), not only was manufacture introduced into the weaving process; going further, even a transition to mechanized production can be recognized in the silk-reeling process. Marx referred to the era when manufacture was the predominant form of capitalist production methods prior to the launch of machine industries in Western Europe as the "manufacturing period, properly so-called," and at the very latest one can safely look upon the late Edo Period, i.e., the years from 1830 onward, as such a period. In assuming such a phase of spontaneous development during the late Edo years, it becomes optimally possible to explain the fact that major machine industries were realized early on in Japan and enabled modernization at a rapid pace not seen elsewhere.

In response, Takao Tsuchiya refuted Hattori's contentions in works such as *Tokugawa jidai no manyu-*

fakuchua (Manufacture in the Tokugawa Period), *Bakumatsu manyufakuchua no shoronten* (Controversial Points in Late Edo Manufacturing) and *Tokugawa jidai no orimonogyō ni okeru ton'yasei kanai kōgyō* (Capitalist Domestic Industry in the Textile Industry of the Tokugawa Period). His argument was as follows.

Tsuchiya contends that the operating mode characteristic of industry during the Edo Period, i.e., the mode of industrial capital, was far more advanced than has conventionally been thought. On this point, he says that Hattori's view is generally acceptable, but he says it is inappropriate to consider the late Edo Period as a "period of manufacture proper." To begin with, as a common rule the capitalist modes of operation prior to mechanization divide into three types:

1) Handicraft industries in which the boss uses hired workers in place of, or together with, apprentices;
2) Capitalist domestic industries;
3) Manufacturing.

Among the three, Tsuchiya argues that the time when the third predominates over the first two constitutes a "period of manufacture proper." In light of such numerous examples as silk reeling, textiles, brewing, wax-making, whale meat processing, minting and metal refining, the number of manufacturing industries is not insignificant; but, Tsuchiya indicates, there are virtually no examples of large-scale manufacturing as seen in Western Europe, and division of labor is at only a modest level.

Small-scale manufacturing operations abound, and only relatively few assign domestic labor to outside departments. Insofar as the silk-reeling and textile industries are concerned, in which manufacturing is said to have reached its highest level of penetration, Tsuchiya states that although manufacturing had reached a fair level of development in some regions, on the whole capitalist domestic industry was the chief mode of operation.

From the foregoing, we see that Hattori's view leans toward theoretical examination in line with the theories of Marx and Lenin, while Tsuchiya's argument is distinguished by its provision of numerous materials.

Subsequently, the manufacture controversy unfolded with both Hattori and Tsuchiya winning supporters of their respective views. As it unfolded, however, participants in general tended gradually to take the view that the economy of the late Edo Period remained still in the phase of small production and small operation, i.e., in an undeveloped state — a view that both Hattori and Tsuchiya had rejected prior to the start of their controversy.

Views of Marx and Lenin

As the manufacture question was raised by Marxist historians, it is necessary to advance our thinking in line with the theories of Marx and Lenin. By developing our view in theoretical order, we should arrive at an understanding of the distance separating Hattori and Tsuchiya, and of the distance separating both of them and the others who entered the debate with their own opinions; and we should be able to measure how appropriate each of their arguments is.

Marx spoke of three forms of capitalist production: co-operation, defined as a relatively large number of laborers working together at the same place at the same time; manufacture, which equates to co-operation through division of labor, in other words, factory-based handicraft industry; and machine industry. Lenin too referred to three forms of capitalist production: small industry, manufacture, and machine industry.

Between them, they differ only in their respective definitions of the first stage, with Marx defining it as co-operation and Lenin, as small industry. On the subject of co-operation, Marx offers this explanation:

"Co-operation…does not, in itself, represent a fixed form characteristic of a particular epoch in the development of the capitalist mode of production. At the most it appears to do so, and that only approximately, in the handicraft-like beginnings of manufacture, and in that kind of agriculture on a large scale, which corresponds to the epoch of manufacture."
— *Translation by Samuel Moore and Edward Aveling, page 287*

Alternately, he says:

> *"Co-operation ever constitutes the fundamental form of the capitalist mode of production; nevertheless, the elementary form of co-operation continues to subsist as a particular form of capitalist production side by side with the more developed forms of that mode of production."*
>
> —*Loc. cit.*

From this we can conclude that co-operation is a comprehensive concept that includes manufacture as well as machine industry.

What Lenin calls "small industry" differs again, being a form that is separate and independent from the other two. According to Lenin, small industry is primarily small-scale agricultural operation that produces for a market; also referred to as "small commodity production," it depends on handicraft skills and uses only a very small number of hired workers. As examples of small industries, Lenin cites iron smithing, shoe-making, hat-making and jewelry-making. According to Marx's way of thinking, industries of this nature do not fit into the category of co-operation, and therefore they are not forms of capitalist production but rather should be categorized as earlier feudal production modes.

Aside from this difference between co-operation and small industry, another point that draws attention with respect to Marx and Lenin is the fact that they do not incorporate the form known as "capitalist domestic industry" into their sequence of development. Marx understands it in a close and inseparable relationship and calls it the underlying basis, the broad background, of manufacture.

"(M)anufacture was unable, either to seize upon the production of society to its full extent, or to revolutionise that production to its very core. It towered up as an economical work of art, on the broad foundation of the town handicrafts, and of the rural domestic industries."
—*Ibid., page 318*

"(T)he manufacturing period, properly so-called, does not succeed in carrying out this transformation radically and completely. It will be remembered that manufacture, properly so-called, conquers but partially the domain of national production, and always rests on the handicrafts of the town and the domestic industry of the rural districts as its ultimate basis."
—*Loc. cit.*

With Lenin, capitalist domestic industry is attendant to all three production forms.

"Capitalist domestic industry—i.e., the processing at home, for payment by the piece, of raw materials obtained from an entrepreneur—is also met with…in the small

peasant industries....(I)t is met with again (and on a large scale) alongside the factory, i.e., large-scale machine industry. Thus, capitalist domestic industry is met with at all stages of the development of capitalism in industry, but is most characteristic of manufacture. Both the small peasant industries and large-scale machine industry manage very easily without domestic industry. The manufactory period, however, of capitalist development...can be imagined with difficulty, or hardly at all, without the distribution of home work. [In Western Europe also, as we know, the manufactory period of capitalism was distinguished by the extensive development of domestic industry — in the weaving industries for instance.] And the facts of Russia do indeed show ...that in the industries organised on the lines of capitalist manufacture the distribution of home work is particularly widespread."

— *University Press of the Pacific edition, page 446*

Measured against the foregoing yardsticks of Marx and Lenin, directly speaking Hattori's contention — that Japan in the late Edo Period was in a manufactory phase — is the victor. This is because during that period broad-based development of handicraft industries was seen in the cities and of domestic industries in the farming villages; moreover, manufacture also appeared, although not in great quantity, thus making this a "period of manufacture proper." However, Tsuchiya's contention actually says something similar. Tsuchiya sets himself apart from Hattori in beginning his argument from three phases of the capitalistic mode of operation based on common sense. He concludes that the late Edo Period "saw a fair amount of development of manufacture, but in general capitalist domestic industry was the prevailing form"; and since that situation was none other than the manufactory phase spoken of by Marx, Tsuchiya's only problem is his terminology—his insistence on using the term "capitalist domestic industry." In essence his argument is not all that different from what Hattori says. Surprisingly, the gap between Hattori and Tsuchiya is extremely small.

Positioning of Capitalist Domestic Industry

Capitalist domestic industry broadly divides into three types or phases: a form in which only products are purchased from small producers, a form similar to that with the addition of provision of advanced loans, and a form in which workers are loaned tools and materials to produce with and provided with wages. In Japan's weaving industry, these three generally correspond to the distinctions among independent weavers, weaver-suppliers and wage-earning weavers. Degree of independence as a direct producer decreases in that order, and with the third type the interpretation can be made that work is distributed due to insufficient land for factories; in terms of its essential quality as labor, it is no different from hired labor performed in one factory (manufacture). In addition, if it is the norm that manufacture cannot be carried out in one factory and capitalist domestic industry is embraced as an outside department, then manufacture and capitalist domestic industry are in many instances intertwined in terms of configuration and difficult to differentiate.

The reason Marx and Lenin did not count capitalist domestic industry as a phase of capitalist production is likely because they stressed labor performed at the same time in the same location; but qualitatively, greater stress should be placed on the factor of hired wage labor. In addition, since capitalist domestic industry has a unique landscape different from other forms of capitalist production operations, it would seem reasonable to incorporate it as a phase and arrive at, as Tsuchiya says, the three phases of capitalist domestic industry, manufacture and machine industry. But, capitalist domestic industry is far closer to manufacture than Tsuchiya believes. Bücher, introduced earlier, places capitalist domestic industry, rather than manufacture, at the fore and accords it major treatment, seeing capitalist domestic industry in the same view as manufacture, with capitalist domestic industry predominating and manufacture in a subordinate role. Dobb says that capitalist domestic industry has nothing in common with the "old-fashioned" domestic industry that preceded it except the name, and that capitalist domestic industry, along with manufacture, constitutes a new mode of capitalist production distinct from the feudal production mode.

In some quarters, capitalist domestic industry is disparaged, and these detractors say capitalist domestic industry is subordinate to commercial capital and is merely a form of industrial domination by forces external to production. This argument is not necessarily on the mark since, firstly, capitalists were not limited to town merchants but, both in Europe and in Japan, at times they were village entrepreneurs themselves (as in the case of weaver-contractors in the weaving industry). Second, and most importantly, this argument cannot avoid criticism for its failure to recognize the emergence of new production modes, i.e., production subordinate to capital in general, and conflicting collaboration between capitalists and wage laborers.

Examples of Late Edo Manufacture

Many instances of late Edo manufacture occurred in the textile industry.

In the 18th century the silk industry differentiated three processes — silkworm raising, silk reeling and weaving; and as technology marked progress in each of these areas, production got under way of commercial products. In the area of silk reeling, while earlier the operational norm was to rent out boiling vats and have the thread reeled off-site, with the invention of a hand-reeling apparatus driven by gear or belt in the mid-18th century, manufacture type operation became widely possible. There is even an example, found in Jōshū (in today's Gunma Prefecture), of a silk-reeling factory that employed 30 female workers simultaneously operating a large number of such apparatuses driven by waterwheel. In the area of weaving, manufacture type operation got under way early in the region around Kiryū and Ashikaga, and it is said that around 1770 there were seven dormitories for workers who supplied the weaving houses, roughly 700 such workers in number, and anywhere from 20 to 200 looms in operation per weaving house. In the Nishijin quarter of Kyoto, although in some cases manufacture was carried out for all three processes, in most instances individual processes were consigned to outside departments and cloth was woven by domestic laborers.

In the cotton industry also, from early on market-oriented production took place under a system encompassing four processes: cotton cultivation, spinning, dyeing and weaving. In Bushu (corresponding to today's greater Tokyo area) around the 1830s, in one example weaving thrived at a workshop equipped with 120 looms and more than 300 indigo vats, to the extent that several hundred of its apprentices or apprentices of apprentices went into business for themselves under its name. In Mikawa (today's eastern Aichi Prefecture) also, during the late Edo Period there appeared roughly 15 indigo dye houses, some of which employed upwards of 15 workers in a system of manufacture. In the area around Osaka, which is known as a region where a commodity economy developed earliest on, during the 1830s 85 percent of the residents of Uda-Ōtsu village were engaged in the cotton industry, as weavers, wage-earning weavers, day-labor wage-earning weavers, etc. There were 18 weaving houses, 10 of which worked exclusively in the weaving business; it is said they employed 82 wage-earning weavers and five apprentices, and many are said to have engaged in capitalist domestic industry type production employing an additional several hundred wage-earning weavers working at home. In the Bisei area (corresponding to western Aichi Prefecture) also, already in the first half of the 18th century manufacture prevailed, and while the majority of producers possessed upwards of six looms, a considerable number of weavers are said to have engaged 10 workers or more.

The foregoing are only a very small sampling of the numerous examples of manufacture cited as having existed in the textile industry. Elsewhere, manufacture is also said to have taken place in industries such as those producing sake, soy sauce, oils and fats, salt, wax, foils and paper, as well as iron smelting.

Many of those who enter the debate about late Edo manufacture conclude that this period as a whole had not reached the manufactory stage. They do so citing the fact that compared to capitalist domestic industry, examples of manufacture were relatively few, plus the fact that a basis for manufacture's development did not fully exist. Tsuchiya, with his theory on the capitalist domestic industry phase, is one who draws that conclusion, but Marx contended, as cited earlier, that (a) manufacture thrived as an economic product resting on the broad base of handicraft industries in the cities and on domestic industry in the farming villages, (b) the 18th century was a century of commerce, and (c) manufacture had only a secondary meaning. Since this is the "period of manufacture proper," this thriving of capitalist domestic labor in the late Edo era fits such a description perfectly. There is no need to make a great issue out of either the number of members of the bourgeoisie deriving from manufacture or the scale of operation.

The idea was also put forward that since capitalist domestic industry equates to commercial capital being dominant over small industry, the late Edo Period was thus a phase of small industry. But small industry consists of isolated, dispersed small-scale operations, and insofar as it lacks elements of concentration and organization, it must be considered fairly remote from capitalist domestic industry. To bring together and organize disparate entities is an imposing task. Also, in opposition to this small industry theory, another theory was put forward that saw the late Edo Period as a "period of manufacture in a limited sense" that can develop into and be linked with the period of manufacture proper;

however, this is nothing else but the period of manufacture proper itself. Another view known as the "wealthy farmer manufacture theory" is of the same kind, for it refers to capitalist domestic labor of wealthy farmers in villages; this notion is close in content to England's operation by affluent farmers (yeomen).

The commonly accepted theory is that in Western Europe between the 16th and 18th centuries, even in England, which was its most advanced corner, what prevailed was a system of capitalist domestic industry built upon broad-based commodity production, in which manufacture had only modest weight of importance. The landscape that typically comes to mind when one speaks of a manufactory period, i.e., manufacture points scattered across hilly districts, is not admitted. According to Dobb, in England from the 17th through latter half of the 18th centuries, capitalist domestic industry, rather than factories or handicraft industry factories, was the typical form of production, and manufacture—including the renowned woolen mills of Winchcombe, Dolman and Stumpe—was of only meager importance within the nation's overall economic life.

Seen in this light, England of the 17th and 18th centuries approaches Japan of the late Edo Period all the more. There may or may not be a spread between the volumes of capital and hired laborers employed in manufacture in such English industries as weaving, mining, salt production, papermaking and ironworks in those days and the corresponding volumes used in those same industries in late Edo Japan. What is of importance here is not such volumes but rather the qualitative similarities in these new economic types: the facts that, in both, (a) countless capitalist domestic industries emerged and (b) among these were scattered examples of manufacture.

In this way, whether considered in the light of Marx's writings, or seen in line with the actual situation of Western Europe that lends support to those writings, and all the more when similarities in background social conditions cited above — production of large volumes of commodities, widespread distribution, flourishing of urban commerce and industry, land annexation, flows of peasants into cities, etc. — are taken into consideration, late Edo Japan qualifies as a period of manufacture proper, and therefore it must be said to be in essence a modern capitalist economic phase.

Early Capitalism and Developed Capitalism

Modern capitalism is the term normally used to indicate, as a whole, the economic system of Western Europe after the 16th century. However, there are also a substantial number of people who take the Industrial Revolution of the latter half of the 18th century as a dividing line, use the term "early capitalism" to indicate what came before it and "developed capitalism" to indicate what came after it, and thus equate modern capitalism primarily, or largely, with developed capitalism. My foregoing indications of the modern capitalist nature of ancient Rome, Han Dynasty China and late Edo Japan are based on the former understanding; but obviously, if one takes developed capitalism characterized by mass production at large mechanized factories as a yardstick, a different case applies, and modern capitalism must be said to have occurred only once in Western Europe.

In such a case, however, a problem that arises is whether or not a yardstick exists for sharply distinguishing developed capitalism from early capitalism. Those who underscore developed capitalism point to various new phenomena that appeared in the developed capitalism phase: not only mass production in large mechanized factories but also thorough rationalization of economic life, strong business intentions, widespread adoption of contract type business modes, the principle of free competition, legal order that guarantees freedom, the spread of joint-stock companies, development of credit, trading in securities, production for speculative purposes, class struggles between capitalists and laborers, etc. Others, however, argue as to whether or not these can be said to be completely new phenomena, and to my mind also, they seem to be qualitatively a continuation of early capitalism and signify a leap in quantity only.

Of course, those who view modern capitalism as one, and who see its essence already in early capitalism, would likely not immediately accept my foregoing view. In reference to the ancient Roman economy, they would probably say: "Wasn't the leading role played by commercial capital?" Also: "Above all, doesn't the fact that it was a slave operation make it fundamentally different from a modern economy?" Or with respect to the Han Dynasty: "It was an economy centered on itinerant commerce, and laborers in an industrial operation could hardly be equated to modern free laborers." As to late Edo manufacture: "The weakness of its foundations can be known also from the fact there are many examples of their vanishing immediately after the opening of ports to the outside world, with formation of industrial capital still extremely young and weak, and it should be said to have lacked the strength to develop into modern capitalism on its own."

Among the foregoing arguments, I contend that I already criticized those projected evaluations. What I wish to discuss, once again, is the core of modern capitalism. The fact that that core was formed in multiple societies is of great importance. By "core," I mean an industrial operation that uses the commodity of purchased labor; rationality, in my view, encompasses it on its perimeter, and machine production and large markets exist further outside. As to the degree to which free labor is involved at the core—and this is most problematic—here I wish to avoid rushing to any conclusion.

What I find odd is that although there are many

people who share the same opinion at least insofar as the core portion is concerned, and although, in addition to the existence of this core there are also similarities in their social backgrounds, cores other than that of Western Europe have traditionally been treated as mere buds. If they are buds, then buds they are—and one must ask why these buds came into being. Particularly as concerns the economy of late Edo Japan, in spite of this amazing example, found nowhere else in world history, of an economy that clearly demonstrates similarities with the early capitalism of Western Europe, comments to date have at most been indications of its manufactory aspect; no one has ever inquired what its significance in world history might be.

This situation is likely attributable to the facts that (a) we are incorporated into the framework of European civilization and European normalities are our common wisdom, and (b) attention is drawn to the exterior view of the developed capitalist society in which we live today. Needless to say, in order to make an objective and fair judgment, it is necessary to break through such temporal constraints and to cast a gaze on the present from a distance.

Conclusion

My task was to identify the power that set modern capitalism in motion in Western Europe.

At the outset I provisionally stated that the power was the Faustian spirit or a rationalist inclination, adding, however, that if modern capitalism exists in plurality, then either we must also recognize a Faustian spirit or rationalist inclination within societies other than Western Europe, or we must conclude that modern capitalism was set in motion in Western Europe by some other force. After examining the economies of ancient Rome, Han Dynasty China and late Edo Japan, I conclude that of those two possibilities, not simply one but actually both apply.

The only way to figure out what causes are behind modern capitalism's plurality as well as behind similarities that exist in the various factors surrounding that plurality, is to adhere to the view that societies develop in parallel. In the preceding chapter I suggested that feudalism emerged as one phase within the course of history of the major civilizations. By the same token, I also view modern capitalism within the framework of the major civilizations and believe that it is the natural point at which that historical progression terminates. Specifically, I see feudalism as a phenomenon arising in the period that centers on the third phase of a major civilization and capitalism as a phenomenon occurring in the period that centers on the fourth and final phase, the age when a civilization became a global power: e.g., the days of the Roman Empire for Greco-Roman civilization, of the Han Dynasty for Chinese civilization, and of the Edo Period for Japanese civilization. In another example of a major civilization, in India too, after passing through the preparatory era encompassing the preceding Maurya and Kushan periods, the ensuing Gupta Empire is said to have been a period in which cities flourished, commerce and industry developed as never before, and guilds of merchants and artisans developed in great variety. In Sumerian civilization, it is said that handicraft industry developed during the period when cities arose independently and vied against each other, and that commerce and industry flourished remarkably during the period of global power opened up by Sargon the Great. Of course, this phenomenon is not true without exception among all the major civilizations, for there are no indications of any flourishing of a private economy in Egypt or Peru. The historical progression of major civilizations is a movement that comes to completion on its own by trending in such directions as technical progress, rising productivity, flourishing of cities, commercial and industrial growth, individualism, underlings toppling their "masters," religious retrogression, intellectual growth, and the accumulation of material wealth. The appearance of modern capitalism, with its commercialism and rationalism, during that final phase is altogether suited to the nature of that movement. This is why modern capitalism exists in multiple civilizations; modern capitalism in Western Europe is only one example.

In this way, the response to the question pending is that modern capitalism in Western Europe was above all a natural product engendered by the history of Western European society, and when the fierce Faustian spirit inherent in Europeans was added in, it led to the discovery of the New World, colonial rule, the Industrial Revolution and the emergence of developed capitalism. As the point may also be argued that the historical dynamics of major civilizations include a self-expanding Faustian quality, the development of Western European capitalism can be said to derive from the synergy of two Faustian spirits.

The foregoing is thus my conclusion; but I wish to touch upon several points that can be deduced as a result.

What if, for example, Western Europe had not had the enormous wealth found in the New World or if Protestantism had not existed? The response to these interesting hypotheses is, one can deduce, that even without these factors Western Europe would still have developed modern capitalism at least to a degree exceeding other societies. Also, what if Japan had had absolutely no contact with Western Europe? One can reply that even so Japan would likely have developed modern capitalism on the strength of its domestic market alone. However, since the inherent nature of Japan cannot be said to be the Faustian spirit, it can be imagined that even if Japan had favorable conditions such as being blessed with overseas markets, it still could not have developed to a form of developed capitalism of the kind seen in Western Europe today.

The question as to why a capitalist structure immediately follows feudalism has far more basic and important meaning than questions of the kind just posed. This is a question that can be adequately answered only from the perspective of the major civilizations, and I believe I have provided that response in this and the preceding chapters. My response is that the causes for the transition from feudalism to capitalism cannot be adequately derived based solely within feudalism as has traditionally been the case; one must look at the overall history of a civilization including periods that preceded feudalism.

A similar situation applies to arguments put forward concerning the reasons for the success of Japan's drive to modernization. Max Weber proposed that the contractual nature of feudalism nurtured Western-style individualism in Japan. Edwin Reischauer (1910-1990) and Joseph Strayer both suggested that feudalism in Japan cultivated points that worked advantageously in the formation of a modern civil society, e.g., the concepts of obligation and justice. In my view, the main reason is to be found more distant and deeper, within history as a whole. In a nutshell, it is the fact that Japan's domestically engendered modernization and externally derived modernization occurred at precisely the same time. As a footnote I might add that Strayer also suggested that

Japan's tradition of modeling itself on Chinese culture may have facilitated its imitation of the West. I would refute that suggestion, however, with the argument that there are many other cultures that had traditions of modeling themselves on foreign cultures. At the same time I also think one must keep fully in mind that Japan's dependency on China, like the West's passionate modeling itself on Greco-Roman culture for more than a millennium, was a creative dependency.

CHAPTER FOUR

Transcendent Sovereignty

— Unraveling the Conundrum of the Emperor System —

Introduction

Feudal society can be seen as society in which anarchy is latent, or as society in a situation close to anarchy wherein the authority of a sovereign ruler has declined, numerous independent forces have arisen in parallel, and internecine struggles are waged among those forces in tests of their respective powers. This view notwithstanding, the fact remains that throughout all feudal periods monarchs whose powers were only equal to, or at times even below, those of their rival forces nonetheless maintained absolute authority. In Western Europe, the Eastern and Western Frankish Kingdoms — in other words, the kings of Germany and France — continued to rule over other lords as unique consecrated secular authorities. In Japan, the Emperor never lost his position of majesty even during the Warring States Period and during the Edo Period when the Tokugawa shogunate reigned supreme—times when real Imperial power withered to nothing.

Why?

The common-sense reply, because the monarch is the center of the state, is not immediately acceptable in the case of medieval societies, which, unlike ancient or modern states, one might even say were not states since their functions as states were paralyzed and they lacked coherence as states.

The controversy surrounding this matter began early in the postwar era, when Tadashi (also, Sho) Ishimoda (1912-1986), a scholar of Japanese history, refuted the argument put forth by the aforementioned Yuzo Horigome. It has continued down to the present within the academic realm of Japanese history, where, in the sense that the matter deals with Japan's *tennōsei*, i.e., Emperor system, it thus has not lost contemporary significance. Concisely stated, the controversy pits the view based on the continuation of the sovereign authority of a pre-existing state outside the feudal structure against the view that sovereign authority was demanded out of necessity within the feudal structure. On the whole, the latter view appears to have been the more persuasive and more widely supported.

Here, my intent is to add in other societies to supplement the materials that have traditionally been compared, which have been limited to those of Western Europe and Japan, and from that broader perspective I will take a fresh look at the question in an attempt to arrive at an answer. In doing so, I will approach the conundrum surrounding the Emperor system from a new perspective, a process that I expect will give rise to a new variety of response. To begin, I will present an outline of the controversy as it has been carried out until now.

1

The Views of Horigome and Ishimoda

Yozo Horigome (in his *Chūsei kokka no kōzō* [The Structure of the Medieval State], 1949, and *Hōkensei no saiseiki to wa nani ka* [What is the Golden Age of Feudalism?], 1952) says that in the medieval feudal states of the West, ultimately the monarch was able to transcend feudal hierarchic relationships and maintain power over other lordly authorities because he possessed traditional authority stemming from a pre-existing unified state. Horigome writes that because of the existence in medieval states of a supreme power at the center of an extant unified state, even if it was no more than a mere spiritual authority, feudalism took the direction of transforming itself into a political organization for manifesting that authority. He further writes that although medieval states were actually as weakly unified as imaginable, in medieval times there was still latitude, even if it was minimal, for states to form: latitude consisting of the monarch's traditional authority beyond anyone's reproach. It was within the scope where the propriety of that authority was believed, Horigome suggests, that comprehensive human groups archetypically formed.

In contrast to Horigome's view that monarchic transcendence is attributable to a power external to feudalism, Tadashi Ishimoda (in his *Chūsei kokka ni tsuite* [On the Subject of the Medieval State], 1950) refutes that argument from the perspective of Japanese history. In Japan, he writes, throughout the medieval feudal period the authority of a monarch—the Emperor—existed, and the feudal state known as the *bakufu*, headed by a military warlord, existed only in the form of the warlord's being appointed by the Emperor, even if only perfunctorily, as "barbarian-subduing generalissimo"—a title more commonly known as "shogun." As to why, among numerous other elements of antiquity, monarchic authority continued to exist as clearly as it did—and did so, moreover, throughout the feudal period—Ishimoda offers the following explanation. Because, he says, feudalism's hierarchy inevitably encompassed exclusive struggles within the vertical relationship of domination/subordination between vassal and lord and within the horizontal relationship of parallel equality among feudal lords, in order for the feudal structure not to collapse under these incongruities a warrior chief—the *bakufu*—functioning as a "non-feudal" unifier and the authority of the Emperor system were both required in feudalism's "laws of motion." In this case, the Emperor system, i.e., monarchic authority, was not merely a leftover relic or just a "non-feudal element"; rather, out of the incongruities in these two relationships it arose and reproduced itself, and in this sense the Emperor system, i.e., monarchic authority, existed as a requisite factor of feudalism.

Horigome accepts Ishimoda's counterargument (which is seen to be derived from Engels' thinking as described in his *Der Ursprung der Familie, des Privateigentums und des Staats* [The Origin of the Family, Private Property, and the State], 1884) as an appropriate criticism of the blind spots in his own view. Citing Max Weber's observation that the reason powerful vassals did not break their relationships with their estates (*lehen*) is because maintaining the ruler's dominant authority served as a basis for justifying maintaining their own fiefs, Horigome then says that the demand for a guarantee of justification was based on what Ishimoda calls the incongruities in the vertical and horizontal aspects within feudalism. However, Horigome goes on to say that Ishimoda's reproduction theory is only logic covering half the whole, and he continues to support his own theory of pre-existing conditions as comprising a "more important half." "Even if medieval monarchic authority was reproduced as a necessary conclusion to the internal incongruities within feudal hierarchy," he writes, "it was not the result of free creation carried out by feudalism on its own, but rather a historical given, a transcendent value largely external to feudalism bestowed from above. Therefore, feudalism, in utilizing this transcendent sovereignty to configure its own order, did not merely reproduce only those parts that it required, but also had to simultaneously incorporate logic inherent in monarchic authority that made it necessary for feudalism to regulate itself."

The View of Sera

Another historian who opposed Horigome's view was Terushiro Sera (1917-1989). Sera endorses and bolsters Ishimoda's view citing passages by Heinrich Mitteis (1889-1952) and Frank Stenton (1880-1967). In his *Lehnrecht und Staatsgewalt* [Feudal Law and State Authority, 1933], Mitteis wrote that when everything is shaking and collapsing, no one can feel powerful enough to get by on his own strength. For feudal individualism to function completely, he said, what was needed was a villain, a contractual counterpart to whom one could foist obligation to the extent one's interests permitted and mutually, on the other hand, on whose aid one could count, depending on the circumstances.

In this way, Mitteis suggested, the feudal pyramid had to forge its own apex from within. Frank Stenton was quoted from his *The First Century of English Feudalism, 1066-1166* (1932). Stenton wrote that there was only one way to escape from a situation of warfare: by becoming subordinate to a dominant monarch by right of lineage, i.e., by unassailable right. Sera further attempts to shatter the remaining half of Horigome's logic, the notion that monarchic authority was a traditional authority passed on from a pre-existing state. Sera contends that the strong conceptual stability of the authority of the monarch actually compensated for what was really extreme instability of the monarch's position, and that it was ideological dressing to infuse stability to the maximum extent possible.

The foregoing is an overview of the controversy that began with the view espoused by Horigome. But, as we will see below, even after the venue of the dispute shifted to Japanese historical studies, it continued to be a debate between whether transcendent sovereignty was an inherently given authority or something that was reproduced.

2

The View of Toyota and Yasuda

Takeshi Toyota (1910-1980: *Chūsei no tennōsei* [The Emperor System in the Middle Ages], 1952) and Motohisa Yasuda (1918-1996: *Hōken jidai ni okeru tennō* [The Emperor during the Feudal Period], 1952) both make statements to the same effect: namely, that while the authority of the Emperor in medieval times was required to guarantee the legitimacy of rule by dominant powers including the Muromachi shoguns, that authority derived from the respect toward the Imperial House that inherently pervaded widely throughout the general populace. Besides the fact that the Imperial Court was the religious and political authority ever since Japan formed as an ancient state, another reason for this was a cultural reason: because the superiority of Kyoto's aristocratic culture centered on the Court had for a very long time sustained the Imperial House's position as a source of honor among the general population. The widespread respect exhibited toward this ancient authority is said to have led to various developments, including: (a) increasing pilgrimages to Ise Shrine as a result of the spreading worship, starting from the 14th century, of the deities from which the Imperial House descended, enshrined at Ise; (b) the use in medieval times by merchants and members of the handicraft industries of documents of approval received from the Court as the basis for receiving special privileges; (c) the view held by *daimyō* warlords all around the country that receiving a rank of peerage from the Court was their supreme honor, coupled with frequent monetary contributions to the Court; and (d) modeling of the warrior code of etiquette, under the *bakufu* system also, on the corresponding code of the Court, and possession by *koke*, nobles who oversaw the *bakufu*'s ceremonies, of higher authority than other *daimyō*.

The Views of Watsuji and Tsuda

The popular respect for the Emperor stressed by Toyota and Yasuda had been emphasized by Tetsurō Watsuji in *Nihon rinri shisōshi*, where he cites examples taken from the Noh theater and popular illustrated literature of the Muromachi Period. In the so-called "god plays" that open Noh performances — or example, *Yumi Yawata* and *Mimosuso* attributed to Zeami (1363-1443) — Watsuji says one finds a fictitious world in which the Emperor reigns over the entire country, in complete contrast to the separation of individual states characteristic of the period, and the Emperor is identified as a deity. This creative posture is carried on in the production of subsequent god plays, and is all the more strongly apparent in works written after the Ōnin War. Emperor worship is also salient in stories written during this period—*Hachiman no Gohonji, Kumano no Honji* and *Mishima*, among others—and in these stories majesty and splendor are all expressed using images relating to the Imperial House.

This way of thought traces back even further to the views on the Imperial House expounded by Soukichi Tsuda (1873-1961). In his *Nihon no kokka keisei no katei to kōshitsu no kōkyūsei ni kansuru shisō no yurai* [The Origins of Thought Concerning State Formation in Japan and the Permanence of the Imperial House, 1946] Tsuda states that already in antiquity the Imperial House was, by virtue of its traditional religious authority as well as its leadership position in new culture based on its introduction of the products of Chinese civilization, a familiar and honorable entity for those holding central powers and for powerful families in the outerlying regions, and by depending on the Imperial House they maintained their lives and positions and satisfied their needs. He adds that when such a situation continued over a prolonged period, the fact that it had continued for so long came to be seen as the essential character of the Imperial House, and the fact that its origins were no longer known induced people to think of the Imperial House as a naturally existing entity—a belief that generated in them a sense of obligation to ensure that it would continue to exist well into the future also. Eventually, Tsuda contends, the center of culture shifted away from the Imperial House to the warrior class and Buddhist temples, and then later to the general populace; but even then, the Imperial House and the residual traces of old culture lingering around it became a target for the classically focused thinking of the learned. The fact that the Imperial House was "above the clouds" charmed the hoi polloi, while feelings of sympathy, sentimentality and poetic pleasure were aroused in the learned; and this, Tsuda concludes, came to form one aspect of the people's view toward the Imperial House.

The View of Nagahara

From the standpoint of one who sees the monarchic authority of the Middle Ages as a living continuation of the authority of antiquity, the contention that this is an apparatus newly devised to resolve the contradictions within feudal society is readily admissible by way of subsuming within oneself the notion that it may also be an apparatus that resolves contradiction by virtue of its being a traditional authority. On the other hand, however, from the standpoint that it is a new apparatus to resolve contradictions, it is not something that can be easily admitted because to recognize traditional authority not only conflicts with one's own view but also runs the risk of being swallowed up by the party making such a contention. This is why, besides being based on fact, Ishimoda and Sera sought to flatly reject the view of Horigome; and as we will see below, it also appears to be one reason why Keiji Nagahara (1922-2004) severely lashed out at the views of Tsuda, Watsuji, Toyota and Yasuda.

According to Nagahara (in his *Chūseiteki seiji keitai no tenkai to tennō no ken'i* [Developments in Medieval Political Formats and the Authority of the Emperor], 1952), the ancient authority of the Emperor possessed real power and significance only until the beginning of the Kamakura *bakufu* era. The situation changed drastically after the Jōkyū War of 1221, which was a rebellion by forces representing the ex-Emperors against the regents of the Kamakura shogunate. The subjugation of Imperial authority is eloquently bespoken by the subsequent treatment accorded to all three ex-Emperors, separation from the old legal order via the formulation of the Jōei Formulary (1232), and the outright rejection by the *bakufu* government of the nobility's demand to restore the ex-Emperor. The same direction is indicated by the wording found in contemporary works such as *Taiheiki*, a historical epic that criticized ex-Emperor Godaigo for what it said was his "complete arrogance and lack of a true sense of justice," and *Jinnō Shōtōki* (Chronicles of the Authentic Lineages of the Divine Emperors), a historical book that castigated Godaigo saying, "revered though His Majesty might be, heaven will not tolerate how he seeks pleasure only for himself and allows the masses to suffer." Furthermore, the discussion raised in *Jinnō Shōtōki* concerning the so-called "sacred treasures," i.e., the belief that the Emperor is divine by virtue of his possession of the three sacred treasures, signifies an escape from reality: namely, the quest for the source of authority in abstract "treasures" in the wake of the real Emperors' loss of their authority. In this way, after the Nanbokucho War, a nationwide upheaval that pitted the Southern and Northern Courts against each other in the mid-14th century, the traditional authority of the Emperor collapsed; however, as feudal forces grabbed power and proceeded to establish a solid position as new rulers, the authority of the Emperor that had temporarily lost its political life was reborn as a necessary factor of a feudal state. The primary purpose behind Ashikaga Takauji (1305-1358) having meted out heavy punishment to military commanders such as Sasaki Dōyo (1306-1373), Toki Yoritō (d. 1342) and Kō no Moronao (d. 1351) for their disrespect toward the Imperial House, and behind Ashikaga Yoshimitsu (1358-1408), despite being in a position to abolish the Emperor system, having instead sought to enter that system and to personally become a retired Emperor, was to be a feudal lord and exercise control over the *daimyō*.

In this way, after initially stressing that the authority of the Emperor collapsed after the Nanbokucho Period, i.e., in the mid-14th century, and was subsequently reborn, Nagahara proceeds to refute the views that had been expounded by Toyota, Yasuda, Watsuji and Tsuda, as follows.

First, in response to the argument that Noh plays treating the Imperial House as a source of honor indicated respect and worship of their Emperors by the masses, Nagahara states that one should not forget that Zeami served the "Imperialized" Yoshimitsu; and he said that the praises sung in Noh chants of an Imperial age of peace and nationwide unity should be interpreted as symbolic of the reign of Yoshimitsu, who brought the Southern Court to its knees, achieved national unification, and transmuted himself into an Emperor. Next, concerning the argument that popular illustrated literature depicted prosperity and worldly success as images connected with the Imperial House, Nagahara states that it was actually altogether natural for worldly success, a revolutionary concept for the masses under feudal rule, to be portrayed as a dream of advancement in the guise of traditional authority; and, he says, at a stage when the masses were unable to make an issue of real power themselves, taking this form was a natural progression. Furthermore, Nagahara dismisses the suggestion that weight was accorded to documents of authorization issued by the Emperor to merchants and factory operators as out of the question because they were members of guilds under the protection of temples and shrines destined to be overwhelmed by new traders. Also, in conjunction with the brisk pilgrimages of worship made to the Ise Shrine, Nagahara opines it is rash to see this as an expression of admiration of and respect for the Imperial House, and he contends this should rather be interpreted as an expression of the contemporary masses' quest after an atmosphere of liberation against the backdrop of their growth both economically and socially. Nagahara points out that this was a period when farmers rapidly began to be liberated from semi-antiquated patriarchal domination, when they became involved in a monetary economy, and when, together with the collapse of the estates, they expanded into commercial businesses transcending narrow regional frameworks, and from these aspects too this was thus a period that sought the removal of checkpoints and freedom of travel. Nagahara suggests that the masses sought to express their rejection of a dominating structure and their expectation of a formation of a mass solidarity in the act of leaving the confines of their villages and traveling to Ise.

Nagahara's overall conclusion is this. The traditional authority of the Emperor, he says, was actually completely reborn throughout the medieval era for the purpose of ruling, and in the true sense it had neither been maintained as a tradition, nor did affection toward the Emperor of the kind suggested by Tsuda spontaneously arise and exist among the populace. Rather, Nagahara concludes, the Emperor system at all times existed only in conjunction with the reactionary side of the feudal rulers, who attempted to use it to obstruct national unification and to utilize their own feudal authority to divide and rule the nation.

Although refutation of Nagahara's criticisms would not seem overly difficult, no one took the initiative to speak out, and the issues that had been raised were left to rest. Debate surrounding the Emperor system in medieval times reignited a decade after the foregoing arguments transpired in the early 1950s, when Toshio Kuroda (1926-1993), in his discourse of 1963 titled *Chūsei no kokka to tennō* [The Emperor and the State in the Medieval Period], introduced his *kenmon taisei* theory, marking a new perspective in Japanese historical studies.

The View of Kuroda

Kuroda advanced the view that alongside the two concepts of *ritsuryō taisei* and *bakufu taisei*—respectively, the system of legal codes used to express Japan's state system in antiquity and the aforementioned shogunate system used as an expression defining the modern state—a concept expressing the Japanese state in medieval times has traditionally been missing, and to express that concept he advocated using the term *kenmon taisei*. *Kenmon taisei*, which literally means "system of powers," refers to a system in which three powerful forces—courtiers and aristocrats, major temples and shrines, and warriors—neither vie against one another nor depend on each other compromisingly, but rather share in administration of the state by relying on and complementing one another institutionally: the courtiers and aristocrats overseeing the promulgation of laws and regulations, appointments and dismissals of bureaucrats, etc.; the major Buddhist temples and Shinto shrines upholding the state through the performance of religious rituals; and the warriors protecting the state through police and defense duties. The Imperial Family, while constituting one power within the category of courtiers and aristocrats, is generally regarded as the greatest among those powers and thus as the source of the state's monarch: the leader who governs over state affairs and represents the state power. In this case three aspects are observed in the Emperor: as a private force in the form of a powerful family, as a systemic ruler exercising state powers, and as a conceptual authority ruling as monarch.

The special character of the Emperor during medieval times becomes clear by tracing how these three powers changed over the centuries starting from the late Heian Period, when the *kenmon taisei* began, through the Kamakura Period, and ending in the late Muromachi Period, when the system came to its denouement. What one finds in doing so is that the Emperor maintained the foregoing three elemental aspects until the early Kamakura Period; then, in the wake of the Jōkyū War the aspect as a powerful family weakened and ultimately collapsed with the split that occurred in the Imperial lineage (between the Daikakuji and Jimyōin lines). The Emperor's aspect as a monarch overseeing all state affairs continued, however, and the Ashikaga *bakufu* was a federation of the various powers centered on the Emperor as systemic monarch. Before long this aspect also weakened, and after Ashikaga Yoshimitsu it became a nominal entity, a form having lost its substance, and ultimately only the authority aspect of the Emperor remained. It did so, as Ishimoda says, because the feudal ruling class needed a traditional authority rooted in antiquity; and the progress seen in the philosophical organization of the temples and shrines, the diversified development of Shinto theology and the widespread dissemination of the notion of a "divine nation" were also nothing but products of religious, ideological measures to sustain the kenmon taisei.

Together with the demise of the Muromachi *bakufu*, however, the *kenmon taisei* effectively ceased to exist, and the Emperor too lost his restricted position and authority as monarch. Under the Edo *bakufu*, as a result of political strategizing the status of the Emperor was restored to fulfill the role of a source of authority, and in modern times, viewed from any perspective, the Emperor was not a monarch at the apex of the political power structure but rather a figurehead in terms only of its relevance to ceremony and ritual. As such, the *kenmon taisei*, i.e., the system in place during the Kamakura and Muromachi *bakufu* eras, is considered to be something applicable only to the medieval period, and by its special nature it should be differentiated from the system under the Edo *bakufu*.

The above is an outline of Kuroda's *kenmon taisei* theory. What is remarkable about this theory is that, unlike the conventional view that treats the medieval warrior-ruled government as a force in opposition to the nobility-based government centered on the Emperor and regards it as the sole embodiment of medieval state power and authority, Kuroda places both the warriors as well as the nobility and religious institutions within a system of divided state duties in which the Emperor is positioned at the top. In other words, Kuroda's theory gave rise to the view that the ancient political structure centered on the Emperor sustained its vitality far longer than conventionally claimed.

Keiji Nagahara, in his *Chūsei kokkashi no ichimondai* [A Problem in Medieval State History, 1964], gave high marks to Kuroda's *kenmon taisei* theory for the way it opened a new perspective in future historical studies. However, he expressed criticism of the theory saying that by considering the court nobility and warriors, traditionally seen as heterogeneous classes, as homogeneous ruling classes of equal rank, it might become difficult to grasp turning points in historical development. He added from the conventional standpoint that the power that propelled medieval history forward was the struggle for state power and authority waged between the nobility and the warriors, and he said it was possible to recognize the *kenmon taisei* system centered on the

Emperor through the Kamakura Period, but in his own view during the Muromachi Period, especially after Yoshimitsu, both the authority and power of the Emperor completely disintegrated and the Ashikaga shoguns were the monarchs holding all state powers. This contention of Nagahara's is repeated in two of his subsequent works: *Nihon hōkensei to tennō* [Japanese Feudalism and the Emperor, 1976] and *Zenkindai no tennō* [The Premodern Emperor, 1979]. As his basis for seeing the era of Yoshimitsu as the starting point of a new epoch in the state system, Nagahara offers three factors: (1) the breakdown of the *shiki* enfeoffment order as estates came to serve as residences of their owners, resulting in the powerful families owning *shiki* in name but not in substance; (2) the absorption of old local state administrative structures into the authority wielded by warriors in the name of *shugo*, i.e., military governors; and (3) the complete concentration of state sovereignty into the hands of the shoguns, coupled with the fact that policy toward Ming China was carried out without any involvement of the Emperor.

These are the main points of Nagahara's counterargument to Kuroda; and although a rebuttal by Kuroda followed, there is no need to spend more time on their exchanges here. This is because the theories advanced by both Nagahara and Kuroda are considered to be extremely close to one another within the overall spectrum of theories expounded on the Emperor system, including those of Tsuda, Watsuji, Toyota and Yasuda. Both Nagahara and Kuroda espouse the same view insofar as recognizing a state system centered on the Emperor through the Nanbokucho Period and seeing its artificial rebirth in the authority accorded to the Emperor in the Edo Period. Where they differ is in reference to the Muromachi Period, especially the years after Yoshimitsu, only. One contends that during this time the Emperor's power became nominal and only his authority survived, while the other holds that both the Emperor's power and authority evaporated during this period and it was the authority that was subsequently reproduced. Thus, the differences between the two scholars are not very significant. Moreover, both Nagahara and Kuroda, rather than seeing monarchic authority after the Middle Ages as a tradition from antiquity, coincide in their fundamental stance that attempts to view that authority as a man-made reproduction targeted at resolving the contradictions and conflicts between the ruling classes, as claimed by Ishimoda; and in this respect they are far apart from Horigome's type of view. However, at least insofar as matters outside the core of their arguments are concerned, Kuroda's view, which sees ancient power as having survived relatively longer, can clearly be said to be closer to the arguments set forth by Tsuda and Horigome. Two theories that are potentially even closer in that direction are the views of Yoshihiko Amino (1928-2004) and Masato Miyachi (b. 1944) described below.

The View of Amino

Amino, in his *Chūsei ni okeru tennō shihaiken no ichikōsatsu* [A Consideration of Imperial Sovereignty in the Middle Ages, 1972], undertook a study of historical materials on various non-farming populations (metal casting workers, woodworkers, medicine peddlers, itinerant vendors of rice, fish, charcoal, etc.) chiefly between the late Heian and early Kamakura periods, and he revealed that these populations undertook their trades by way of special privileges granted to them by the Court and nobility. Amino states that these non-farming populations formed professional groups, affiliated themselves with specific powerful forces and, equipped with formal documents of authorization issued by the Emperor or central government agencies, traveled and traded freely in all states, regardless of rule by specific feudal lords. Amino then examines the source of the Emperor's sovereignty over transport routes — the "vascular tissue" of that society — and he conjectures that it originated in the Emperor's inherent sovereignty over the "earth and seas" by virtue of his being the community chieftain, and that in tandem with progressive private division of all land and waters from the 8th century onward, Imperial sovereignty came to be expressed in the form of the granting of rights of free passage.

Although Amino's study was essentially an extension and expansion of what Toyota and Yasuda had pointed out, as described above, concerning the guarantee of special privileges via the documents of permission granted to commercial entrepreneurs in the late medieval era, his work in itself did not raise any new issues and by its nature was not controversial because it is applicable up until the early Kamakura Period. Since according to Nagahara the Emperor's authoritative rule continued until the Nanbokucho Period and according to Kuroda it extended even further, to the latter half of the Muromachi Period, it is thus commonly agreed that at the time Amino is addressing, Japan's entire national territory was the Emperor's domain.

The problem lies in the situation of the non-farming population after Yoshimitsu, which Nagahara sees as a time when both the power and authority of the Emperor evaporated. To date, however, a detailed and comprehensive study of this matter has never been undertaken, and only occasional indications are found that the circumstances of this time period continued subsequently also. Regarding Amino's view, however, although Nagahara states that it would be problematic if Amino were to make the same contention with reference to the late medieval period because this would mean considering Imperial rule as substantive, he nonetheless says that while he thinks it is an incontrovertible fact that the relationship between the professional groups and the Emperor for the most existed in the Warring States Period also, it is necessary to ascertain somewhat more specifically whether or not a relationship of that kind did indeed seamlessly continue. Moreover, Nagahara says that because the relationship between the "non-farming populations" and the Emperor state system formed in the early medieval period, together with its accompanying mode of consciousness, forms a historical undercurrent, the "official" rule of the Warring States *daimyō* needed to take a form in response to it, and thus unable to assemble logic flatly denying the Emperor, the *daimyō* took the direction of using the traditional state system to the maximum extent possible. This is a way of thinking that allows for a continuation of the preceding period and thus runs counter to Nagahara's own theory. This probably owed in no small way to the study carried out by Masato Miyachi which, as described below, leaped over the Muromachi and Warring States eras and dealt with the situation of artisans during the Edo Period.

The View of Miyachi

According to Miyachi — as described in his *Chōbaku kankei kara mita bakuhansei kokka no tokushitsu* [Distinctive Features of the Shogunate-Domain State from the Perspective of the Relationship between the Shoguns and the Court, 1975] and *Bakuhansei-ka no kan' i-kanshoku seido* [The System of Official Ranks and Posts under the Shogunate-Domain System, 1976] — during the Edo Period the artisan class as a whole (including foundry workers, carpenters, makers of official attire, producers of paper for official documents, sculptors, armor makers, lacquerware makers and decorators, blacksmiths, acupuncture practitioners, saddle makers, seal carvers, inkstick and inkstone makers, confection makers, mirror makers, street vendors, etc.) sought to elevate their social privileges through court ranks received from the Emperor. As an example, nearly all foundry workers nationwide were under the rule of the Matsugi family, who were in charge of the Court's document bureau, and from them they received their ranks. Whenever there was a change in the family's leadership or succession within the ranks of the foundry workers, it was mandatory for a trip to be made to the capital to have the change approved. Any time a new Emperor took the throne, again a trip had to be made to the capital in order to offer congratulations and labor service, while at normal times—New Years, harvest festivals, etc.— the foundry artisans were required to offer up gifts of thanks to the Matsugi family. Similar remarks can be made with respect to other professions also. Within the circles of the nation's medical practitioners, two families (Nakarai and Imaoji) that held posts as principal court physicians occupied the highest ranks among doctors within the *bakufu* office system, and beneath them was a pyramid of physicians of lower ranks bestowed by the Court (*hōin, hōgen, hōkyō*). The world of artists too was configured like a pyramid: at its apex were the Tosa and Kano families, who were originally painters exclusively in the service of the Court, and under them were artists of various rankings (again, *hōin*, *hōgen* and *hōkyō*) bestowed upon them by the Court. Shinto priests, fortunetellers and sumo wrestlers were also connected to certain powerful families and received ranks and documents of authorization from the Court. Blind individuals who made their living as musicians, masseurs or money lenders belonged to a hierarchic system of appointed professions (four *kan*, 16 *kai* and 73 *koku*) headed by the Kuga family. Miyachi uses materials such as these to support his contentions that (1) the power of the Court originally permeated down to the smallest "capillaries" of society, (2) for that reason *bakufu* rule would not have been possible without the Court's existence, and (3) only by enfolding the Court and making use of it was the *bakufu* able to exercise nationwide authority.

This is also indicated clearly in Miyachi's description of how the various domains were assigned state tasks (construction of bridges, riverbank, etc.) and how temples were dominated—facts which he uses as material for considering how political rule during the modern shogunate state of the Edo Period differed from during the medieval *bakufu* state of the Muromachi Period. He shows that although state tasks, centering on construction of the palace, seemed on the surface to have lost their meaning during the Warring States Period, they actually were revived during the Edo Period to a strong degree not seen during the Middle Ages. Also, whereas during medieval times the warriors and religious institutions were both subordinate to the Court as powerful forces independent of one another, the Edo *bakufu*, after a fierce struggle against the Court, ultimately secured rights to rule over the religious institutions; however, upon doing so, the *bakufu* was unable to acquire independent authority, and in order to dominate over the nation's temples and shrines it had to utilize the system of Court appointments of ecclesiastical authorities that had been employed continuously since the age of the *ritsuryō* system.

Based on facts such as these, Miyachi concludes that the Court (1) was a necessary constituent element of the state, as known from various appellations applied to Japan with the character for "Court" in them (*honchō, kōchō*); (2) was a presence deeply ingrained in the state consciousness not only of the warrior class but also of the general population; (3) set in place the status system applied to the entire population; and (4) not only possessed religious authority but also, as an entity in charge of educational functions, had a fixed position within the shogunate state, and the *bakufu* maintained official power in its inseparability from it. This conclusion of Miyachi's can actually be seen to work to the advantage of the theories advanced by Tsuda, Watsuji and Horigome, but his accompanying comment seems to stand, conversely, on the side of Ishimoda and Nagahara. What Miyachi contends in the latter case is that although today it is widely viewed that the Emperors in feudal times exercised no power but enjoyed wide support from the masses, actually, as just described, the Emperors and Court functioned as an important part of the feudal state effectively enough to wholly rule over the masses. His conclusion, however, clearly seems to substantiate that a living traditional authority continued to function through the Edo Period—a contention flatly denied by both Nagahara and Kuroda.

3

A Problem Point in the Debate

The foregoing is an overview of the debate surrounding transcendent sovereignty, in particular the transcendent power and authority of Japan's Emperors during medieval times.

One facet of this debate that raises misgivings is the lack of absolute logical clarity regarding the point at the center of the debate. The difference between saying that transcendent sovereignty is traceable to a given power, i.e., traditional authority, and seeing transcendent sovereignty as a reproduction stemming from creation, can be seen as a difference between whether the given traditional authority continues to exist or whether it is defunct. The only participants in the debate who clearly say that the authority has completely died out are Keiji Nagahara and Toshio Kuroda; virtually all proponents of the reproduction theory eschew clarifying any specific dividing line between that authority's life and its death and, if anything, seem to speak of its continuing usage as a living power. The difference here is substantial, for whereas in the case of Nagahara or Kuroda they contradict and reject those who take opposing views, the other members of the debate are able to harmoniously coexist with their opponents. As to whether or not it is possible to artificially revive authority that has completely perished, I believe that it is more reasonable to think that new vigor can be created relying on a modicum of remnant vitality; reproduction of authority that has perished completely is no more than a pole of logic placed at the antipodes of the functioning of traditional authority itself. I think that only one thing is feasible in reality: the maintenance and usage of traditional authority by artificial revitalization, on each occasion, of vitality descending infinitely toward that pole.

Viewed from this point, the essence of this debate reveals itself to be not a conflict between one point and another, but a matter merely of a difference of degree on a commonly shared line. If those who join the camp advocating the reproduction theory would exercise self-awareness, they should come to realize that so long as they embrace this usage theory, their position is surprisingly close to that of their opposing camp. As such, I offer that before proceeding with the debate it is necessary for them to think these matters over. Even the argument regularly used by those who take this position as a trump card against those of the opposing view—i.e., that the masses, because of their immaturity, were always linked to and held within the grasp of feudal rulers by means of political intentions—does not go beyond the scope of this usage theory.

4

A New Approach

Next, I will consider the matter using the two materials already discussed, Japan and Western Europe, plus two new materials: China and Egypt. I am adding the two new materials because, like Japan and Western Europe, China and Egypt are also societies that experienced feudalism and sovereign transcendence during their respective feudal periods. What I aim to do is, using these four materials, to attempt to elucidate the matter by a new approach. Specifically, I will seek to clarify the circumstances of the emergence, flourishing and decline of their sovereign power and authority, as well as the essential nature of that power and authority common to all four societies, by comparing and mulling their respective histories rather than the arguments based on specific historical evidence as described above. Once these clarifications have been achieved, I will then apply them to explain transcendent sovereignty.

The Cases of China and Japan

First, I will take up the cases of China and Japan.

In China, periods when transcendent sovereignty was in evidence are the Spring and Autumn and Warring States periods. Similarities can be recognized between the situations of those two periods as well as of the periods prior and subsequent to them, and the situation of Japan during its corresponding eras.

During the Spring and Autumn Period the House of Zhou gradually lost real power, and after the arrival of the Warring States Period it came to exist virtually in name only. Nonetheless, for five to six hundred years, until it was obliterated by the Qin, the House of Zhou continued to reign over the feudal lords with what may be called "inviolable" authority. This closely resembles the situation of the Imperial House of Japan in the four to five hundred years between the late Heian Period and the beginning of the Edo Period.

The general circumstances of the periods of China and Japan in which monarchic power and authority declined and of the periods prior and subsequent to them also have many significant points in common. First, they were periods of upheaval when war continued to rage between feudal forces. Second, during these periods the spread of iron wares and progress in technology led to increased agricultural production capability, commercial and industrial advances fueled the gradual adoption of a money economy, and cities emerged around the nation. Third, subsequent to these periods powerful states emerged (Han and Tokugawa *bakufu*) and sustained peace. Fourth, prior to these periods there arose centralized, unified states (Western Zhou, Nara Period). Fifth, four or five hundred years earlier, in both China and Japan there were states, tribal federations in their nature, in which monarchic power and authority were still weak (Yin, Tumulus Period); also, these are periods viewed as having marked the start of subsequent long-enduring periods clearly separate from the periods that preceded them (Yangshao and Longshan cultures, Jomon and Yayoi cultures).

Next, I will compare the two countries in greater detail, focusing only on the rise and fall of sovereign power and authority. At the time of their foundation as unified states, sovereign power and authority were strong in both Japan and China. In Japan, that power and authority weakened after one hundred and fifty years, in the mid-9th century, when governing power and authority passed into the hands of the Fujiwara regents. Similarly, in China, according to the previously introduced *Shi*

Ji, after one hundred or one hundred fifty years, during the fifth Zhou reign, i.e., that of King Mu, kingly power and authority weakened and fighting began among the feudal lords. Although that decline deepened with the passage of time, the House of Zhou, like Japan's Imperial House, continued to be revered by the feudal lords, including the de facto rulers at specific times. This sustained reverence is recognizable from a variety of facts, including (1) pacts to uphold the House of Zhou that were entered on numerous occasions at meetings of feudal lords, (2) handing down of titles of victor by the House of Zhou, (3) joint dispatches of troops by feudal lords to fight attacks by barbarians against the Zhou, and (4) collective construction of the Zhou capital cities during the reigns of King Jing and King Ding. Furthermore, even during the Warring States Period, when the House of Zhou is said to have plummeted to its lowest point, during the reign of King Xian (368-321 BCE) Qin summoned the feudal lords to Zhou and made them pledge their loyalty, and the Qin king received his title as victor from the House of Zhou, holder of the "Mandate of Heaven."

As this indicates, actual monarchic power and authority in China and Japan during their respective feudal periods, as well as the peripheral historical situations surrounding them, were surprisingly similar, and by comparison the differences between the two societies are negligible: for example, the fact that the House of Zhou, unlike the Imperial House, was a lord-like power ruling over its own territory, or the fact that in China there existed no equivalent to Japan's *bakufu*, i.e., no political structure around which various forces assembled.

In China, did the power to sustain this sovereign transcendence derive from traditional authority as a given, or from a man-made authority reproduced for the purpose of averting anarchy? Based on the previously introduced *Zuo Zhuan* and *Shi Ji*, what we find are records all appearing to support the former view.

To cite an example, the passage describing events in the fifth year of the reign of Duke Huan of Lu (late 8th C BCE) states that when the Earl of Zheng stopped offering tribute, the king led an army of allied forces from Cai, Wei and Zhen and attacked Zheng, but in the end they were defeated and the king himself was injured. The general whose shot had caused injury to the king offered to launch a punitive attack, but the Earl of Zheng would not allow it. "To recklessly vanquish even an ordinary human being is something that a man of virtue would not do; how much more when it is the Son of Heaven we are speaking of. As my state is safe and our divine sanctuaries secure, that is sufficient." The Earl of Zheng then dispatched a messenger to inquire of the king's retainers how he was faring.

Again, in the passage relating events in the ninth year of the reign of Duke Xi (mid-7th C BCE), which discusses the Kuiqiu oath, the Marquis of Qi at one point refused to show his respects to the Son of Heaven by stepping up to where his lord was waiting. "I cannot possibly pay my respects directly before His Majesty," the Marquis said. "If I were to impertinently accept the invitation to do so, I might well stumble and do dishonor to His Majesty's authority." He therefore remained a level below and stepped up to receive the gifts bestowed upon him.

In the twenty-fifth year of the reign of Duke Zhao (late 6th C BCE), a meeting of representatives from the various states was convened at Huangfu, where it was decided that to assist the House of Zhou they would all send rice and establish an army of defense. The envoy from Song refused to send rice, however, on the grounds that Song was a "guest" of Zhou. The envoy from Jin retorted, "Ever since the alliance at Jiantu, Song has taken part in all wars and cooperated in all alliances. You also swore to join us in keeping the House of Zhou's interests at heart, and now you want to break that promise? You are participating in this important meeting upon the orders of your lord. Wouldn't it be untoward for Song to turn its back on the alliance?" The envoy from Song is said to have been at a loss for words, and he bowed and took his leave.

What merits notice here is the conspicuous preponderance in *Zuo Zhuan* and *Shi Ji* of records of the feudal lords swearing direct loyalty to the House of Zhou and the near total absence of records that would suggest they viewed the House of Zhou as an entity existing to function as a guarantee of the legitimacy of their own rule or to avert chaos. The descriptive manner employed too is redolent with sentiments of awe and allegiance. To weigh historical facts based on historical or literary works, one must collectively take into consideration a variety of elements, including the recorded content, writer, reader, ruler and the society as a whole. Just as one must be alert to demands from above, i.e., from the ruler, one must consider demands from below, i.e., from society. Accordingly, while it may be hasty to immediately conclude that the foregoing records demonstrate the sustainment of a traditional authority, by the same token it would be hasty to immediately conclude that they indicate only a rebirth of authority. If one views both arguments as issues of possibility, I believe the correct answer is to situate the transcendent sovereignty of the House of Zhou on the line seen earlier, a considerable bloom of the inherent vitality of traditional authority.

According to the *Shi Ji*, just prior to the House of Zhou's demise, when Qin attacked Zhou, the Prince of Zhou reportedly said to the King of Qin: "For the King's own sake, it would be best not to attack Zhou, because even if you attack Zhou there would be nothing of benefit. The news that you had attacked the Son of Heaven would strike fear in the hearts of everyone throughout the land, and if the whole land became fearful of Qin because of this hearsay, everyone would inevitably drift eastward and join with Qi." Again, in the *Zuo Zhuan* whenever there is mention of dissension within the House of Zhou, or discord between the House of Zhou and the feudal lords, or struggles among the feudal lords themselves, the same scene is frequently depicted: namely, a remonstrator appears and instructs the dissenters on the true kingly way or the way of being a loyal subject, citing the example of what happened when King Wu invaded Yin or King Ping moved his capital to the east. Both instances surely indicate that even after the monarch's power had weakened, its traditional authority remained intact.

The Case of Egypt

Next, to turn to the case of Egypt, transcendent sovereignty is discernible in the time frame between the late Old Kingdom and the establishment of the New Kingdom. Where similarities with Japan and China exist is in the gradual fragmentation of public power to local feudal forces—lords of provinces referred to as "nomes"—and the progressive weakening of the effectiveness of a central administration, followed by a transition to a period of anarchic upheaval in which entities wielding real power collided, a situation that continued for several hundred years. Two other similarities can be found in peripheral historical situations. First, after the transitional period there emerged a powerful empire that sustained a lasting peace (the New Kingdom: 1580-1100 BCE). Second, prior to the transitional period there was a centralized, unified state (the Old Kingdom: 2700-2200 BCE); and before that, there had been a period lasting five hundred years (the Early Dynastic Period, encompassing the First and Second Dynasties: 3200-2700 BCE) during which sovereignty was weak and states consisted of tribal federations—a period seen, by dint of the commencement of a dynastic system and of a system of writing, as the harbinger of a subsequent lengthy period of culture.

The early part of the Old Kingdom period saw a strong concentration of power into the hands of the pharaohs, as symbolized by the building of the great pyramids in their names (Snefru, Khufu, Khafre, Menkaure). But as a result of the successive construction of temples, exemption of religious institutions from taxation, and the granting of land to powerful retainers, fiscal collapse ensued, and toward the end of the Fourth Dynasty fragmentation began, governors became feudal landlords and broke away from the central government, and official posts at the central level came to be passed on privately by powerful families. These trends became all the more salient as the years passed, and then during the First Intermediate Period (2200-2050 BCE)—which followed the Old Kingdom after it came to its denouement with a clutch of short-lived kings during the Sixth Dynasty—local fragmentation reached a decisive level, the rulers of the nomes took possession of their respective territories, and wars setting one private army against another were waged repeatedly. Taking advantage of this chaotic situation, outside groups undertook successive invasions of the Nile Delta region, until Mentuhotep II, who reigned over Thebes, brought this upheaval to an end and founded the Middle Kingdom. During the first half of the Middle Kingdom (Eleventh and Twelfth Dynasties: 2050-1800 BCE), the locally fragmented structure remained and the nome rulers enforced private rule over their territories, succeeded to titles, and used their own reign names; but during the second half, sovereign power rose up and asserted itself strongly over the local powers, and the reign names of the pharaohs came to be used to define the periods inscribed on tombstones. Most notably, Senusret III internally undertook bold administrative reforms and succeeded in eliminating the power of the local aristocracy; externally, he elevated national prestige by expanding his territorial borders through an invasion of Libya to the west, suppression of Nubia to the south, and a far-flung military campaign against Palestine to the north—achievements for which he was celebrated as the Middle Kingdom's greatest hero. Even during this latter half of the Middle Kingdom era, however, in contrast to the absolute autocracy of the Old Kingdom, maintaining a balance between the power of the pharaoh and that of the regional rulers was critical, and to that extent sovereign power and authority are said to have been limited. After a period of two hundred years the Middle Kingdom ultimately collapsed, once again casting Egyptian society into an abyss of anarchy. Taking advantage of that situation, the Hyksos, who were Asiatic in origin, invaded Egypt and settled in the Nile Delta region. Relying on their superlative military capabilities, they set up their own dynasty and eventually wrested control over the entirety of Egypt, exercising direct rule over the northern and central areas and establishing suzerainty over local lords in the south. This is the tumultuous era known as the Second Intermediate Period (Thirteenth through Seventeenth Dynasties: 1800-1580 BCE), during which the Hyksos were eventually routed by an army raised by Ahmose and Egypt regained independence, ushering in the New Kingdom.

The foregoing describes the changes in the political situation of Egypt during the period at issue. In addition, a number of features have been suggested as barometers of shifts in the psychological situation of Egyptian society: for example, during the Middle Kingdom, the free movement of urban residents from city to city; the emergence of members of the handicraft industries, merchants and *artistes* who accumulated wealth; the development of a refined, urbane artistic sense contrasting with the bucolic rusticity characteristic of Old Kingdom arts; cultural inwardness as expressed in the anguished appearance of the pharaohs or their discernible "humanization" in their sculptures of this era; and a tangible transition toward lighthearted, cosmopolitan elements in the arts and language of the New Kingdom. Such changes in psychological circumstances in some ways resemble the course of history in Japan and China, and in tandem with similarities in political and external changes, they pique our interest.

Where sovereignty in Egypt differs from the sovereignty in Japan or China is in its frequent changes of dynasty. During the respective periods under review, whereas one family line was maintained in both Japan (the Imperial House) and China (the House of Zhou), in Egypt quite a few lines came to rule. If sovereignty can be said to exist either because of the bloodline in its background or by virtue of the throne it occupies, Egypt shows a sustained sovereignty chiefly of the latter type.

The Case of Western Europe

Another society whose historical situation closely resembles that of the three just described is Western Europe. The similarities include the fact that Europe in the Middle Ages — the time when transcendent sovereignty was in evidence — was a feudal society marked by fragmentation of public power; that this was a period of upheaval; and that it was a period during which expanded adoption of iron implements and technological advances drove a dramatic increase in agricultural production, commerce and industry arose, urban centers developed, and a transition got under way from a nature-based village economy to an urban money economy (although the latter few points are not entirely clear with respect to Egypt). Also, prior to the Middle Ages, a centralized, unified state had been formed under Charlemagne; and before that there existed a tribal federation type state (the Frankish Dynasty under the Merovingians) for more than three hundred years, when the base of sovereignty was not yet fully established; and this period is seen as the advent of the long cultural traditions that were to follow it. Two dissimilarities are the facts that the unified sovereignty of the Frankish Empire eventually split in two—the West and East Frankish kingdoms—and that following the period of upheaval in Europe's Middle Ages, there was no powerful, centralized military and police state of the type one would have expected, or it had yet to appear. These dissimilarities seem pale in comparison to the various similarities noted, however.

In the West Frankish Kingdom (France), from its early days local aristocrats (dukes, earls, etc.) wielded great power, and even after the Carolingian dynastic line ended and was superseded by the Capetian Dynasty in the latter half of the 10th century, sovereignty remained weak and the territory controlled by the kings consisted of only small areas around Paris squeezed in between lands owned by the various lords, or isolated enclaves within those lands. The lords held official posts carried on from the Carolingian unified state and were nominally state officials and officers of the king, but they far surpassed the kings in terms of real power. Starting in the 13th century, however, sovereign power joined with urban forces and expanded rapidly, giving rise to a feudal monarchy in which the king exercised control over the entire political order.

In the East Frankish Kingdom (Germany), from the time the Carolingian line expired in the early 10th century, an elective monarchy was introduced; until the mid-13th century, this monarchy was ruled by a succession of dynasties (Saxon [Ottonian], Salian and Staufen), and during this period sovereign power remained relatively strong. However, in polar contrast to developments in France, in the East Frankish Kingdom sovereign power weakened starting in the 13th century, the powers wielded by the lords expanded, and after a long period without any king on the throne in the wake of the demise of the Staufen Dynasty, a transition took place to an era of separate states and no unified state power. One remarkable feature in the case of Germany is the fact that in the latter half of the 10th century King Otto I embraced the ideal earlier held by Charlemagne to revive the Roman Empire, and accepting the crown to the Holy Roman Empire from the Pope, he restored Roman imperial authority. In the Christian world of

Western Europe, coronation signified hegemony, and although subsequently the Kings of Germany, i.e., the Holy Roman Emperors, actually ruled over Germany and Italy only, ideologically for a long time they were the foremost authority in Europe, superior to all other sovereign rulers.

In this way, the time frame in which transcendent sovereignty is an issue is from the 9th to 12th centuries in the case of France, and even longer in the case of Germany. But what merits notice here is the paucity of historical materials, of the kind found in Japan and China, to corroborate that absolute loyalty or allegiance to the emperor or king existed widely in Europe. In Japan, through the Edo Period the Imperial House largely gave the impression of being a religious presence, one often regarded as existing "above the clouds" to be worshiped and loyally followed by its subjects. In China, while the *Zuo Zhuan* and *Shi Ji* may not suggest any sentiments to an equal extent, passionate fealty to the House of Zhou existed broadly for many centuries. Contrastingly, the perception of a monarchic dynasty held by Westerners is quite "human." This is only to be expected in the case of Germany, where emperors were elected from among the lords. Yet even in France, where dynastic pedigrees were an object of respect, kings were on a par with lords and they ruled over small estates only; they were distinguished in standing only by virtue of their having been consecrated by the Church, and the depictions of kings presented in historical materials thus were not those of beings considered to be divine in their status.

Marc Bloch, the French historian (1886-1944), cites the example of kings who, it was believed, possessed the power to cure disease, after which he states the following:

"It would be easy to cast doubt on the effectiveness of this popular conception of kingship by contrasting the marvellous aura which surrounded the persons of kings with the scant respect which was often paid to the royal authority. But this would be to misinterpret the evidence. The examples of kings whose vassals disobeyed them, fought against or flouted them, and even held them prisoner, are indeed numberless. But of kings who died a violent death at the hands of their subjects in the period we are considering there are, unless I am mistaken, exactly three cases: in England, Edward the Martyr, the victim of a palace revolution fomented on behalf of his own brother; in France, Robert I, a usurper slain in combat by a partisan of the legitimate king; and in Italy, the scene of so many dynastic struggles, Berengar I. By comparison with the hecatombs of Islamic history, or with what the West itself could show in the number of great vassals murdered, and considering the general moral outlook of this age of violence, this number seems small indeed."

— *Marc Bloch, Feudal Society, page 381*

For those of us today who are comparing the European situation with the situations of Japan and China, however, if this is the only evidence there is, then what Bloch says would seem to support the general assessment that kings remain within the human dimension, rather than that they approach a divine dimension as Bloch contends. This relative weakness of kings in the Occident is likely connected directly to the fact that, in contrast to the sustained existence of imperial houses outside the feudal system in both Japan and China, the royal dynasties of the West were positioned—as entities *within* the feudal system—at the apex of the hierarchical pyramid formed by the human relationship between feudal lord and feudal subject; but at a deeper level, it is related to racial disposition. Specifically, although the relationship between feudal lord and feudal subject was a lord-vassal type relationship, unlike in Japan and China it was largely a reciprocal relationship between two equal free persons, and although a physical relationship—the bestowal and receipt of feudal lands—had been set in place by virtue of an innately human relationship of domination, circumstances easily became reversed and the physical relationship came to be accorded precedence; and—unlike the Japanese notion that "a loyal subject does not serve two lords"—it was normal in the West to have multiple lords at the same time, a notion characteristically unique to Western European society. From our perspective, it seems fundamentally rooted in the mentality of a race that accords precedence to the individual over the group and that, instead of valuing the solidarity of the group, sees conflicting clashes between the equal rights of individuals as the norm.

When mulling the transcendent sovereignty of the West, clearly, considering how weak that sovereignty was, theories founded on notions of usage or reproduction can easily seem to make sense. As such, one can readily understand how people like Weber, Mitteis and Stenton could attempt to see monarchs only as means of guaranteeing the self-justification of feudal subjects or as mechanisms for averting situations of total anarchy.

5

Identification of Traditional Authority

The foregoing are, to my knowledge, four societies that, at least as discernible from related literature, experienced transcendent sovereignty under feudal systems spanning several hundred years. The fact that a similar phenomenon of this nature occurred in four societies, plus the fact that four societies underwent basically similar historical progressions which, including their respective time frames as well as the periods before and after, spanned lengthy durations, suggests that it is not only feasible but perhaps even necessary to seek the resolution to the problem at hand by mulling the historical courses of those four societies.

Next, therefore, as an approach to understanding transcendent sovereignty itself, I will attempt to identify what traditional authority is, because transcendent sovereignty is a matter concerning the traditional authority that monarchs possessed, regardless of whether one views transcendent sovereignty as a product of traditional authority or as the result of its reproduction.

Yuzo Horigome offered up three elements—Germanic, Christian and Roman—as factors that formed the basis of the traditional authority held by the monarchs of Western Europe during the Middle Ages. Horigome opined that the Germanic element is the oldest and consists of the magical authority vested in the lineage of the Germanic tribal kings. Subsequently this was augmented by the Christian element: God-given authority based on confirmation by the Church of competence worthy of being entrusted with the divine command to rule, which enhanced the king's pedigree further. Finally, the Roman element—the notion of supreme ruling authority stemming from rule over Gaul and restoration of the Western Roman Empire—synergetically served to elevate the original authority. Horigome's study stops at identifying these three factors as the basis of traditional kingly authority; he does not go any further in clarifying what its ultimate source

Transcendent Sovereignty

might be. Terushirō Sera, whose identification of sovereign authority is similar to that of Horigome, also took his analysis no further.

For the most part, what European scholars view as the foundation of sovereignty is a distinct authority based on Christianity: the God-given authority corresponding to Horigome's second element. According to Bloch, sovereignty in France during feudal times was sanctified by the king's taking custody of a sacrament of oil from the Church, vesting in the king a divinity setting him apart from other lords.

> *"From the end of the ninth century the archbishops of Rheims claimed to have the custody of a miraculous oil, brought down to Clovis of old by a dove from the vault of heaven — a wonderful privilege which at once enabled these prelates to claim the monopoly of the coronation and their kings to declare and to believe that they had been consecrated by God himself."*
>
> — *Marc Bloch, loc. cit.*

In reference to imperial authority in medieval Germany, Heinrich Mitteis wrote that imperial power was ultimately based on an entity having transcendence. Mitteis said that the German Empire was a sacred empire possessing a religious, mysterious power, and therefore it needed to be justified through faith. Among Japanese scholars of Western history also, there appears to be a prevailing view that likewise sees Christianity as the ultimate basis of sovereignty in Europe. As an example, one standard history of France (edited by Kōji Inoue, 1968) says that the authority of the aristocracy was justified by the king, and the king's own basis of justification was God. This work states that here the upward directivity in the quest for a basis for justifying authority ultimately reaches its zenith.

I, however, strongly sense that sanctification is no more than a decorative outer covering, and that beneath that covering lies the inherent source of authority. Even with respect to lineage-based power, this can readily be looked upon with suspicion in view of the frequency of dynastic changes. In essence I believe it is no more than ornamentation; it is not the image itself. The third element cited by Horigome—the Roman element—refers to a Roman autocratic element, the absolute nature of the king elevated to transcendence above the community, appended to the ancient Civil Code type element of Germanic kingly power, coupled with the adoption of Roman judicial and administrative systems resulting from the conquest of Gaul by the Frankish tribes, and capped by the restoration of the Roman Empire by Charlemagne. Here too, however, in my eyes this appears to be like a nimbus and not the image it complements. In my view, the image is not these three elements but rather the actual original sovereign authority that Horigome contends was heightened by those elements.

Transcendent Sovereignty

Why does original sovereign authority form the nucleus of the traditional authority wielded by kings?

Original sovereign authority signifies Merovingian dynastic authority. In the early phase of the dynasty's reign, Clovis, head of a branch of the Frankish tribes, founded the Frankish Empire, Western Europe's first multiethnic state spanning a broad territory; society was converted to Orthodox Roman Catholicism; and a state system was established based on the introduction of Roman administrative and judicial systems (founding of a chancery; preparation of official documents; setting out of administrative districts; introduction of bureaucratic and tax/duty systems; establishment of a royal trial court transcending tribal boundaries; etc.). These developments collectively signify Western Europe's departure from a Germanic tribal society and a shift to a new, qualitatively different type of society, as well as a transition from a naturally arisen gregarious way of life to a legally ordered life as citizens of a state: in short, a leap from a primitive society to a civilized state.

Indeed, conventional histories of Western Europe commence with the birth of this kingdom and contend that Western European society was formed starting from this point and that Western European cultural traditions flowed from this original source. This is a point in time that lends itself readily to such depictions as "the dawn of history" or "the beginning of the universe." We frequently come across recorded descriptions giving the impression that the birth of a Western European mentality traced to Charlemagne, not King Clovis; and even in Horigome's aforementioned explanation, King Clovis makes no appearance, being buried among the various kings of the Germanic period; yet the various deeds performed by Charlemagne — territorial expansion, compilation of a legal code, reforms of the currency system and military government, promotion of culture and education, creation of a system of royal itinerant inspectors, and coronation of the Emperor — would seem to be of a character that one should see as an extension, enhancement, arrangement or finish of undertakings by the various kings tracing back to Clovis. Just as subsequently the new dynasty under the House of Capet immediately proclaimed its intention to carry on the traditions of the Carolingians, Pepin, who established the Carolingian Dynasty, and his successors are said to have indicated their intent to carry on the traditions of the Merovingians. With regard to the legend relating to sovereign authority introduced above also, what the story of the alleged custody by the archbishops of Rheims after the ninth century of a miraculous oil brought down to Clovis by a dove from the vault of heaven aims to convey may be directly, as Bloch says, their prized possession of a sacred oil, but on a deeper level it clearly can be read as a paean praising Clovis as Europe's very first king.

In view of the foregoing, I would like to seek the origin of the traditional authority possessed by kings in the sovereign authority vested in the early Merovingian Dynasty contemporaneous with the origin of the traditions of what we know as "Europe," and identify its content as the authority to start a civilized society and rule over it continuously. To my thinking, it is original sovereign authority—in which Horigome did not see any special powers—that constitutes the ultimate and greatest element of traditional authority, and it is around this main body that lineage-based power, religious ceremony and the Roman element attached themselves as ever-expanding adornment. This, I conclude, is the true entity of what we refer to as the traditional authority of kings.

Authority of the Monarch of Civilization

The situation is all the clearer with respect to the other three of the four societies under discussion, for within each of these sovereignty is viewed as having been stronger than in Western Europe. Menes (alternately identified as Scorpion or Narmer), who established Egypt's First Dynasty, King Tang, who founded China's Shang (Yin) Dynasty, and Himiko or Amaterasu, who is considered the progenitor of Japan's Yamato Court, were all monarchs who stood on the cusp between a primitive society and a civilized one; and with each of them a royal lineage commenced that was to endure for one thousand five hundred or two thousand years, advanced cultural traditions began to form, and a colorful history got under way. In all three cases, tracing back over their respective royal lineage, culture and history one ultimately arrives at these monarchs. It was during their respective eras that writing was invented and came to be used, that objective judicial and administrative systems and structures were created, and, particularly in Egypt, that styles of art were established. Also meriting notice—and this is a phenomenon not seen in Western Europe—is the implementation in these respective eras, for the very first time, of large-scale building projects: in Egypt, construction of temples (and later, pyramids); in China, of vast walls and underground tombs; and in Japan, of giant tumuli. The spectacle of these enormous and grandiose structures suddenly appearing on vastly expansive plains undeveloped and primitive since time immemorial was like a landmark commemorating the inauguration of a new, civilized society. Herein lies the original sovereign authority of these three societies, and the content of that authority, as in the case of Western Europe, is understood to be the authority of the monarch of civilization—"the authority to start a civilized society and rule over it continuously." This is interpreted to be the "central axis" of the traditional authority vested in these societies' kings or emperors.

6

Unraveling the Conundrum

Once the nucleus of traditional authority is known, unraveling of the conundrum of transcendent sovereignty is within close range.

An examination of the subsequent course of events within the four societies just introduced, each of which began with a great monarch who opened the way to its civilized development, reveals that they all went on to expand their territory of rule, increase sovereign power while setting systems and structures in place, and gradually, over a span of roughly five hundred years, shed their aspect as a tribal federation type state and proceeded to build a centralized, unified state. However, within the short span of but one or two hundred years, these unified states all began to break down, and after another two to three hundred years monarchic power was virtually depleted, ushering in a period in which local nobility wielded real power and fought among themselves for supremacy. This outcome of political fragmentation likely owed to each society's immaturity in terms of political rule; but in the cultural aspect, developments continued forward across the entire land, with the result that culturally there was no loss of social unity. In this respect, the emergence of fragmented local forces does not represent a regression to a pre-civilized status, but rather can be viewed as a new type of divided rule within the civilization process—a phase we refer to as a "feudal age."

If we now transpose this thinking and focus on sovereignty, given that real sovereign power and authority equate to the power and authority of the ruler of civilization—the ruler who dominates over all areas of human activity within a civilization's advanced cultural phase, including religion, manners and customs, arts and literature, economics and politics—although the disintegration and dismantling of a unified state is accompanied by a withering of political power, it may be said that in other cultural realms the sovereign power and authority continue. This, I believe, is how the transcendence of sovereignty in feudal periods might best be understood.

Civilization and Sovereignty

The historical development of a civilization is a transition from a society centered on one monarch to one centered on an aristocratic minority, and then on a majority of the population. It is a process that begins with those in a subordinate position believing in and following one who is in a superior position, and, after passing through the successive stages of obedience, antipathy and then defiance, ultimately ends in rejection of that higher being. In the context of the relationship between the monarch and the common people, it is a process that begins with the masses personally subordinating themselves to and following a monarch, and ends with their total rejection of that monarch.

In primitive tribal societies, the individual is absorbed into and is an indistinguishable member of the communal society; he is no more than an accidental constituent element that acts in line with society's volition. The unity of the society is substance and god, and the activities of its members are truly acts of faith toward that god. The ancient state is a quantitative extension of this tribal society, and the despot who rules over it is the embodiment of a greater unity consisting of an aggregation of the individual unities of each tribal society; the masses remain submissive to and believe in this divine monarch like appendages of a natural organism. Eventually humans become self-aware, an aristocracy arises, and the unity of the communal society weakens, which accordingly leads to a decline in sovereign power and authority. Next, in place of the aristocracy the masses rise up and grow, engendering a decline in sovereign authority not only within the political sphere but in cultural realms as well, until finally that authority becomes form without substance. In the process, we find the phenomenon of a "humanization" of the erstwhile divine monarch. In Egypt, during the Middle Kingdom the pharaohs underwent a metamorphosis from divine kings to human beings; in Japan, many episodes from medieval times speak of the human nature of Emperors and Ex-Emperors, and members of the nobility criticized them scathingly.

These developmental dynamics of history are discernible only in a limited number of societies, including the four we are addressing here. In other societies — for example, the various kingdoms of East and West Asia — tribal societies remained static and lacked historical dynamism, i.e., they saw no rise of an aristocracy, growth of the masses, decline in sovereign authority, or any other political, economic, social and cultural developments.

In order to gain a full understanding of the authority of the monarch of civilization, in addition to this historical rise and fall it is necessary to comprehend the true nature of civilization. If we were to confine the concept of civilization or advanced culture only to the level of a superficial phenomenon, ultimately it would not greatly transcend the realm of politics.

Civilization, along with being a social revolution, is a revolution in consciousness. Civilization reaches to the depths of human awareness and engenders a new world understanding. Through civilization the world opened up and took on the appearance we see today, and through advanced culture our current existence reveals itself as we are aware of it in the present. Accordingly, the significance of a monarch being not only a monarch of politics but also the monarch of civilization lies in his being the king of existence, lord of the world. Civilization is light, and the monarch who creates civilization is the source of that light. In the formation of a state, light spreads across the firmament; and in the emergence of a unified state, light spreads across the whole land. Sky and earth, mountains and seas, fields and rivers, grasses and trees, rain and wind, clouds and moon, morning and night, light and dark—bathed in this light of life they all cease being materials and become culture.

When a civilized world is viewed this way as a world of a higher dimension, a level apart from primitive society, it is on its golden soil that human life is carried out, political and economic events unfold, artistic activities pursued, class struggles waged, and wars started; here, therefore, total anarchy is an impossibility. The reason the Emperor system is said to permeate down to every blade of grass and the leaf of every tree can be taken as a depiction of this landscape precisely. The reason, too, why people swarm around the Court and compete for ranks and posts, regardless of what it may appear to be on the surface, basically is because they want to verify themselves as being in this dazzling land.

While I do not know how long such a situation continued or will continue, it is probably justified to see it as having continued at least through a time frame including the Edo Period, when society marked sustained coherent development amidst qualitative homogeneity. Tokugawa Mitsukuni (1628-1701) reportedly stated that the Emperor is "our" ruler and the Tokugawa shogun is but the commander in chief of the army. Sir Rutherford Alcock (1809-1897) wrote that the Emperor was "the only sovereign de jure recognized by all Japanese from the Tycoon to the lowest beggar." Such statements are neither contrivances nor hyperbole; they can be taken as expressions of the situation as it truly existed.

What I say applies to all four societies. In Western European society, sovereign power is weakest in terms of its external political clout, and therefore when viewed from the outside, Western European society tends to give the impression that its kings, as Weber and Mitteis said, were entities that existed only for the purpose of offering a basis of justification for the feudal lords. Yet even with respect to that society, my fundamental view is the same as toward Japan. With regard to Egypt also, even though specific materials cannot be found that would enable direct weighing of that society's transcendent sovereignty, I believe that similarities in peripheral historical situations justify seeing the continuance of the supremacy of sovereign authority in conjunction with the advent and continuation of civilized society.

* * * * *

In the foregoing I attempted to unravel the conundrum of transcendent sovereignty by means of comparative history. The attempt was based on my own idea, and if any similar studies by my predecessors exist, I am unaware of them. To summarize from the perspective of the major civilizations that I described in the preceding chapters: the four societies cited are type A societies identical to those that experienced feudalism, as I dealt with in Chapter 2; and transcendent sovereignty invariably accompanies feudalism and its source can be sought in an ancient unified state or in the authority of even earlier great kings of a tribal federation type state at the origin of civilization. Absolute and inviolable divine kings, an ancient unified state covering a broad area, a feudal system, and a decline and transcendence of sovereignty are all brilliant features shared exclusively by type A major civilizations and not found in other civilizations. Individual differences naturally exist among such civilizations, however. As I have indicated, in terms of distinction between modern or ancient types, Western Europe—in which the royal pedigree fragmented and weakened early on, giving rise to developments in new notions including rights of resistance, contracts, freedom, equality and independence—is a classic example of a modern-oriented society. Japan—in which the original purity of royal lineage continues and in most recent times supreme joy was found in restoring the ancient state and submissive subservience to one divine ruler—can be said to be the optimal example of a society oriented toward antiquity. It was surely this antiquated disposition encapsulated, to a considerable extent, in the DNA of Japanese society that in contemporary times enabled Emperor Shōwa (Hirohito) to state in his Imperial Rescript on the Termination of the War in 1945: "May ye, my subjects, hold well the thoughts I hold in my heart."

    (originally published in Japanese in September 1988)

Outline of Japanese History

200-250	Birth of Yamato, a tribal federation state ruled by Queen Himiko
200-700	Tumulus Period
8th C	Nara Period
701	Establishment of the Taihō Code. Inauguration of a unified state
9-12th C	Heian Period
1150-1185	Genpei War. Start of period of upheavals (12-16th C)
12-14th C	Kamakura Period
1192	Inauguration of the Kamakura *bakufu* (shogunate) by Minamoto Yoritomo
1221	Jōkyū War
1333	Demise of the Kamakura *bakufu*
14-16th C	Muromachi Period
1336-1392	Nambokuchō War
1338	Inauguration of the Muromachi *bakufu* by Ashikaga Takauji
1368-1394	Reign of Ashikaga Yoshimitsu
1467-1477	Ōnin War
15-16th C	Warring States Period
1573	Demise of the Muromachi *bakufu*
17-19th C	Edo Period
1603	Inauguration of the Edo *bakufu* by Tokugawa Ieyasu
1867	Demise of the Edo *bakufu*, Meiji Restoration

Bibliography

Chapter 1

Anderle, Alfred et al. *Welgeschichte in Daten* [World History in Data]. Berlin: VEB Deutscher Verlag der Wissenschaften, 1965.

Asakawa, Kan'ichi. "Some Aspects of Japanese Feudal Institutions." In *Transactions of the Asiatic Society of Japan*, XLVI, Part 1, 1918. pp.77-102.

Bloch, Marc. *Feudal Society*. Trans. L.A. Manyon. Chicago: University of Chicago, 1961.

Ganshof, F.L. *Qu'est-ce que la féodalité?* Brussels: Office de Publicité, 1957.

Geschichte 6 (Lehrbuch für 6. Klasse). Berlin: Volk und Wissen Volkeigener Verlag, 1978.

Hall, John. "Feudalism in Japan—A Reassessment." In *Comparative Studies in Society and History 5*, October 1962. p.21.

Hintze, Otto. "Wesen und Verbreitung des Feudalismus." In *Staat und Verfassung*. Göttingen: Vandenhoeck & Ruprecht, 1962. pp.84-119.

Horigome, Yōzō. *Yōroppa chūsei sekai no kōzō* [The Structure of Medieval Europe]. Tokyo: Iwanami Shoten, 1976.

Ienaga, Saburō. *Nihon dōtoku shisōshi* [History of Japanese Moral Thought]. Tokyo: Iwanami Shoten, 1954.

Lenin, Vladimir. *The Development of Capitalism in Russia*. Honolulu: University of Hawaii Press, 1956.

Lyon, Bryce. *The Middle Ages*. Washington: Service Center for Teachers of History, 1965.

Nagahara, Keiji. *Hōken shakairon* [Feudal Society]. In *Chūseishi kōza 5*. Tokyo: Gakuseisha, 1985.

Prawer, Joshua and S.N. Eisenstadt. "Feudalism." *International Encyclopedia of Social Sciences*, Vol. 5. New York: The Macmillan Co. & The Free Press, 1968.

Sera, Terushirō. *Hōkensei shakai no hōteki kōzō* [The Legal Structure of Feudal Society]. Tokyo: Sōbunsha, 1977.

Strayer, Joseph. *Feudalism*. New York: Robert E. Krieger Publishing Co., 1979.

Strayer, Joseph and Rushton Coulborn. "The Idea of History." In *Feudalism in History*. Ed. Rushton Coulborn. Hamden CT: Aachon Books, 1965. pp.4-5.

Tsurumi, Naohiro. *Chūgoku hōken shakairon* [Chinese Feudal Society]. In Chūseishi kōza 5. Tokyo: Gakuseisha, 1985. p.10.

Watsuji, Tetsurō. *Nihon rinri shisōshi* [History of Japanese Ethical Thought]. Tokyo: Iwanami Shoten, 1952.

Weber, Max. *Economy and Society I, II*. Berkeley: University of California Press, 1968.

Chapter 2

Coulborn, Rushton. "A Comparative Study of Feudalism." In *Feudalism in History*. Hamden CT: Archon Books, 1965. p.185ff.

Hintze, Otto. *op cit.*

Tonomura, Naohiko. *Hachi-daibunmei* [Eight Major Civilizations]. Tokyo: Asahi Press, 2008.

Tonomura, Naohiko. *Hikaku hōkenseiron* [Comparative Feudalism]. Tokyo: Keisō Shobō, 1991.

Tonomura, Naohiko. *Tagen bunmei shikan* [A Comparative History of Civilizations]. Tokyo: Keisō Shobō, 1991.

Weber, Max. *Economy and Society II.*

Chapter 3

Bücher, Karl. *Entstehung der Volkswirtschaft.* Tübingen: H. Laupp, 1919.

Dobb, Maurice. *Studies in the Development of Capitalism.* London: Routledge & Kegan Paul, 1946.

Hattori, Shisō. *Hattori Shisō chōsakushū* [An Anthology of the Works of Shisō Hattori]. Tokyo: Rironsha, 1954.

Hilton, Rodney. "Introduction." In *The Transition from Feudalism to Capitalism.* London: New Left Books, 1976.

Lenin, Vladimir. *op. cit.*

Marx, Karl. *Capital—A Critical Analysis of Capitalist Production.* Berlin: Dietz, 1990.

Meyer, Eduard. "Die Wirtschaftliche Entwicklung des Altertums" [The Economic Development of Antiquity]. In *Jahrbücher für Nationalokonomie und Statistik* [Journal of Economics and Statistics], Bd. IX, 1895.

Reischauer, Edwin. "Japanese Feudalism." In *Feudalism in History.* Ed. Rushton Coulborn. Hamden CT: Aachon Books, 1965. pp.46-47.

Sima Qian. *Records of the Grand Historian.* Trans. Burton Watson. Hong Kong: Chinese University of Hong Kong, 1993.

Sombart, Werner. *Der Moderne Kapitalismus.* Leipzig: Dunker & Humblot, 1928.

Spengler, Oswald. *Decline of the West*. Trans. C.F. Atkinson. London: George Allen & Unwin Ltd., 1954.

Spengler, Oswald. *Der Untergang des Abendlandes*. Munich: C.H. Beck, 1923.

Strayer, Joseph. "The Tokugawa Period and Japanese Feudalism." In *Studies in the Institutional History of Early Modern Japan*. Princeton: Princeton University Press, 1968. pp.10-14.

Sweezy, Paul. "A Critique." In *The Transition from Feudalism to Capitalism*. London: New Left Books, 1976.

Tsuchiya, Takao. *Nihon shihonshugi shironshū* [History of Japanese Capitalism]. Tokyo: Ōdosha, 1947.

Utsunomiya, Kiyoyoshi. *Kandai shakai keizaishi kenkyū* [Studies on the Socio-economic History of the Han Dynasty]. Tokyo: Kōbundō, 1955. p.8.

Weber, Max. *Economy and Society II*.

Weber, Max. *Gesammelte Aufsätze zur Religionssoziologie* 3Bde. Tübingen: Mohr, 1920-21. Vorbemerkung.

Chapter 4

Amino, Yoshihiko. *Chūsei ni okeru tennō shihaiken no ichikōsatsu* [A Consideration of Imperial Sovereignty in the Middle Ages]. Tokyo: Iwanami Shoten, 1972.

Bloch, Marc. *op. cit.*

Horigome, Yōzō. op. cit.

Ishii, Susumu. *Insei jidai* [The Age of Ex-Emperors]. In *Nihonshi 2*. Tokyo: Tokyo University Press, 1970. p.217.

Ishimoda, Tadashi. *Chūsei kokka ni tsuite* [On the Subject of the Medieval State]. In *Hōgakushirin* No. 48-2, 1950.

Kuroda, Toshio. *Chūsei no kokka to tennō* [The Emperor and the State in the Medieval Period]. In *Nihon chūsei no kokka to shūkyō* [The State and Religion in Japan's Medieval Period]. Tokyo: Iwanami Shoten, 1975.

Mitteis, Heinrich. *Lehnrecht und Staatsgewalt* [Feudal Law and State Authority]. Weimar: Böhlau, 1933.

Miyachi, Masato. *Tennōsei no seijishiteki kenkyū* [Political History of the Emperor System]. Tokyo: Azekura Shobō, 1981.

Nagahara, Keiji. *Chūsei kokkashi no ichimondai* [A Problem in Medieval State History]. In *Shisō* No. 475, June 1964. p.42.

Nagahara, Keiji. *Nihon hōken shakairon* [Japanese Feudal Society]. Tokyo: Tokyo University Press, 1955.

Nagahara, Keiji. *Zenkindai no tennō* [The Pre-modern Emperor]. In *Rekishigaku kenkyū* No. 467, April 1979. p.37ff.

Nagahara Keiji and Keiji Yamaguchi. *Nihon hōkensei to tennō* [Japanese Feudalism and the Emperor]. In *Rekishi hyōron* No. 314, June 1976. p.2ff.

Sera, Terushirō. *op. cit.*

Stenton, Frank. *The First Century of English Feudalism*. Oxford: Clarendon Press, 1932.

Takeuchi, Teruo, trans. *Zuo Zhuan* (Chronicle of Zuo). Tokyo: Heibonsha, 1972.

Toyota, Takeshi. *Chūsei no tennōsei* [The Emperor System in the Middle Ages]. In *Nihon rekishi* No. 49, June 1952. p.5ff.

Tsuda, Soukichi. *Nihon no kokka keisei no katei to kōshitsu no kōkyūsei ni kansuru shisō no yurai* [The Origins of Thought Concerning State Formation in Japan and the Permanence of the Imperial House]. In *Tsuda Soukichi zenshū* [The Complete Works of Soukichi Tsuda] No. 3. Tokyo: Iwanami Shoten, 1963. p.450ff.

Watsuji, Tetsuro. *op. cit.*

Yasuda, Motohisa. *Hōken jidai ni okeru tennō* [The Emperor during the Feudal Period]. In Shisō No. 336, June 1952. p96ff.

About the Author

Naohiko Tonomura
Born in 1934.
Graduate of The University of Tokyo (Faculty of Letters).
Professor Emeritus of Okayama University.
Area of specialization: Comparative History of Civilizations.

Publications (all in Japanese):
1. *Nihon bunmei no genkōzō* [Protostructures of Japanese Civilization]. Tokyo: Asahi Press, 1975.
2. *Tagen bunmei shikan* [A Comparative History of Civilizations]. Tokyo: Keiso Shobo, 1991.
3. *Hikaku hōkenseiron* [Comparative Feudalism]. Tokyo: Keiso Shobo, 1991.
4. *Sou bunka to tsuku bunka: Nihon no zōkei yōshiki* [Japanese Style of Art]. Kyoto: Tankosha Publishing, 1994.
5. *Datsu-ō nyū-kindai* [Quit Europe and Join the Modern Era]. Hiroshima: Keisuisha, 2003.
6. *Hachi-daibunmei* [Eight Major Civilizations]. Tokyo: Asahi Press, 2008.

Naohiko Tonomura's principal work divides into five categories.
1. With his clear solution faithful to Marx's texts, he put an end to the great international debate, spanning seven decades, surrounding the "Asiatic mode of production" set forth by Karl Marx. (publication #2)
2. Based on an objective guideline, i.e., tracing nearly an identical

About the Author

historical course with respect to phases and duration, he identified eight major civilizations, thereby advancing comparative civilization studies. (publications #2 and #6)

3. He spelled out a precise definition of the concept of feudalism and offered an entirely new interpretation of the causes behind the formation and decline of feudal systems. (publication #3)
4. He proposed an aesthetic theory whereby, using a geometric formula to distinguish two types of art styles (two systems each comprising three conceptual pairs), he clarified that traditional cultures both East and West followed one or the other of the two in their creation of paintings, sculpture, music, performing arts, architecture, clothing, swords and everyday utensils. (publications #1, #4 and #6)
5. He clarified that the "modern era" equates not to the modern era of Western Europe but to the neutral, universal and inorganic civilization first experienced by humankind, and he proposed that through this modern era it is possible for all peoples to live lives rooted in their own culture while respecting other cultures. (publication #5)

About the Translator

Robert A. Mintzer

Born in New Jersey, USA, 1949. PhD, Harvard University, 1978 (East Asian Languages and Civilizations). Freelance translator and copywriter based in Tokyo. Acquired Japanese citizenship in 1995, adopting the name Rei Muroji (室生寺玲).

Please order this book through the bookstore in your country.

Feudalism
A Comparative Study

2011年7月25日 初版発行

著　者	Naohiko Tonomura（外村直彦）
訳　者	Robert A. Mintzer
発行者	原　雅久
発行所	株式会社 朝日出版社

101-0065 東京都千代田区西神田 3-3-5
電話（03）3263-3321（代表）

DTP：越海編集デザイン
印刷：協友印刷株式会社

©Naohiko Tonomura 2011, Printed in Japan
ISBN978-4-255-00599-7 C0082

乱丁・落丁の本がございましたら小社宛にお送りください。送料小社負担でお取り替えいたします。
本書の全部または一部を無断で複写複製（コピー）することは、著作権法上での例外を除き、禁じられています。